POETRY REV

SPRING 1996 VOLUME 8 6

EDITOR PETER FORBES
SUBSCRIPTIONS AND ADVERTISING RAC
PRODUCTION MARTIN DREWE

CONTENTS

Royal Festival Hall
on the South Bank

Poetry Events

Poetry From Pakistan
17 April **Rukhsana Ahmad, Kishwar Naheed and Fahmida Riaz**
Feminism and sexuality examined by three formidable writers

Poetry From Pakistan
18 April **Salman Asif, Iftikhar Arif, Ahmad Faraz and Ahmad Nadeem Qasmi**
Poetry as a popular form and its social and political context

25 April **Paula Meehan and Ruth Padel**
Passionate and moving poems about Ireland

1 May **Kwame Dawes and Geoff Hattersley**
Forward Poetry Prize winner joins slyly funny streetwise poet.

7 May **Seamus Heaney**
New work from the 'greatest Irish poet since Yeats'

9 May **Alice Oswald and Mario Petrucci**
Startling originality which makes the ordinary beautiful

23 May **Eleanor Brown and Alicia Stubbersfield**
Exhilarating flexibility and subtle sensuality

4 June **Miles Champion and Tobias Hill**
Experimental passion and wry observation with an urban slant

18 June **Adrian Mitchell**
One of Europe's bestselling poets whose political work embraces a vital popular tradition

27 June **Charles Boyle and James Lasdun**
Inventiveness and wit shimmering with quick intelligence

Box Office 0171 960 4242
Events take place in the Queen Elizabeth Hall RFH2, Purcell Room RFH3 and the Voice Box.

POETRY REVIEW
SUBSCRIPTIONS
Four issues including postage:

UK individuals £23
Overseas individuals £31
(all overseas delivery is by airmail)
USA individuals $56

Libraries, schools and institutions:
UK £30
Overseas £37
USA $66

Single issue £5.95 + 50p p&p (UK)

Sterling and US dollar payments only.
Eurocheques, Visa and Mastercard payments are acceptable.

Bookshop distribution:
Central Books
Telephone 0181 986 4854

Design by Philip Lewis

Typeset by Poetry Review

Printed by Warwick Printing Co Ltd at Theatre Street, Warwick CV34 4DR and at 112 Bermondsey Street, London SE1 3TX
Telephone 0171 378 1579

POETRY REVIEW is the magazine of the Poetry Society. It is published quarterly and issued free to members of the Poetry Society. Poetry Review considers submissions from non-members and members alike. To ensure reply submissions must be accompanied by an SAE or adequate International Reply coupons: Poetry Review accepts no responsibility for contributions that are not reply paid.

Founded 24 February 1909
Charity Commissioners No: 303334
© 1996

THE POETRY SOCIETY

EDITORIAL AND BUSINESS ADDRESS:
22 BETTERTON STREET, LONDON WC2H 9BU

telephone **0171 240 4810**
fax **0171 240 4818**
email **poetrysoc@dial.pipex.com**

ISBN 1 900771 00 4
ISSN 0032 2156

Funded by
THE
ARTS
COUNCIL
OF ENGLAND

HOW THE CENTURY LOST ITS POETRY

by Peter Forbes

In 1921 T. S. Eliot, with *The Waste Land* written and about to be published, wrote in his essay 'The Metaphysical Poets':

> We can only say that it appears likely that poets in our civilisation as it exists at present must be difficult. Our civilisation comprehends great variety and complexity, and this variety and complexity, playing upon a refined sensibility, must produce various and complex results. The poet must become more and more comprehensive, more allusive, more indirect, in order to force, to dislocate if necessary, language into his meaning.

This idea took hold in an extraordinary way, so much so that when poets began to write more lucidly, about the new industrial and political landscape of the 30s, in the language which we now recognise as the 20th century's own – that is, shorn of Victorian portentousness, ethereality, and rhetorical redundancy – hardly anyone seemed to notice beyond the by now very small circle of committed insiders ("jackals snarling over a dried-up well" – Cyril Connolly). The *myth* of difficulty overcame the actual new lucidity. English poetry as enshrined in Palgrave's *Golden Treasury* went on (confirmed last year in the poll for the nation's favourite poem, when Kipling's 'If' won followed by Wordsworth, Tennyson, Yeats, Keats, Owen, and only Stevie Smith from the mid 20th century); the mad modern poets wrote their incomprehensible poems for each other in little huddles in bohemia, and never the twain did meet. "Never the twain did meet". I consciously used that expression because it represents the old language: it is not the language of the 20th century. Every time until ours has appreciated poetry written in its own accents. So what is the difference between the language before and after 1914? Just before Eliot, poets tended to write like this:

> Or when the wind beneath the moon
> Is drifting like a soul aswoon,

> And harping planets talk love's tune
> With milky wings outspread, Yasmin . . .
> (James Elroy Flecker, 'Hassan's Serenade')

The real revolution actually effected by Eliot and Pound was in diction. When Eliot began to write "The winter evening settles down / with smell of steaks in passageways", he instantly put "aswoon" and its allies out of their misery. But, as Timothy Steele pointed out in his important book, *Missing Measures*, when it came to prescription rather than practice, Pound and Eliot – especially Pound – mistook their target. Pound blamed metre and rhyme for the decay of poetry at the turn of the century ("to break the pentameter that is the first heave"). Equally, Eliot's insistence on complexity now seems wilful and an unwarranted extrapolation from his own extraordinary sensibility.

The fragmentation of metre urged by Pound and the dislocation of imagery enjoined by Eliot were mutually reinforcing. Together they were a very effective pantomime horse indeed. But form is not responsible for diction: Shakespeare didn't produce anything like the etiolated, effete verse of the '90s poets and the Georgians; nor did the formal poets of the 20th century when they got into their stride. The great pleasure of formal verse comes from its dual function, playing off the sounds of sense against the metre, as Robert Frost said. But for Pound the bathwater was so disgusting, any babies in there didn't stand a chance. Modern verse was going to be free verse.

The Waste Land is the poem that justifies Modernism: totally original, moving across a vast panorama of European culture, from high to low – there is nothing like it in poetry. Pound's editing of course enhanced its modernist dislocation and unsupported allusion. It worked triumphantly here, but as a recipe for poets and critics it was a disaster. As Gavin Ewart put it: "Eliot loved the music halls / (and he probably liked pantos). / Pound took the rubbish out of *The Waste Land* / And put it all into the *Cantos*". "Make it new", said

Ezra and so unleashed the permanent avant-garde, because you can be "new" in an arbitrary way without being in any way interesting or meaningful.

Where did Eliot's blithe assertion of the necessity of difficulty in complex times come from? You could just as easily assert the opposite: the necessity for clarity. Obviously, Eliot was only justifying his own practice, but why was it so influential? Largely because difficulty was fodder for the critical industry that began to grow up in the universities after the First World War. University English Studies did not exist at the turn of the century. By the 1920s they were established. And what better than some difficult texts to unravel? Cliques, whether poetic, political, or literary critical, thrive on shared nonsense. Indeed, there is much evidence that because it doesn't matter to the cohesion of the clique whether they deal with sense or nonsense, so long as every one obeys the rules, the currency of such groups tends to become nonsense. Hence the L=A=N=G=U=A=G=E poets in America huddling around texts which are deliberately meaningless to non-initiates.

Or the higher absurdities of literary theory. To see how infuriating the latter can be, try an essay by Richard Rand – 'Ozone: an essay on Keats':* "If I assert for example that 'Keats took a lively interest in ozone', then I commit an anachronism . . . for ozone was first discovered by the German chemist Christian Friedrich Schonbein in 1840, and Keats had already checked out, as the current slang has it, in 1821". Rand pursues the complete lack of connection between Keats and ozone for 14 pages.

Modernism is one of Richard Dawkins' memes. It exerted a powerful form of blackmail – like Christians clinging to belief because of the fear of hell: "it's the safe bet". Modernism claimed to be the only true path. If it was, its opponents risked the total worthlessness of everything they did. Modernism was the equivalent of a malign medieval superstition – striking the fear of Pound into every poetic soul for half a century. In the name of science and progress and permanent revolution it actually enforced a cramping orthodoxy. Similarly, postmodernism today as preached by the theorist of *The New Poetry*, David Kennedy.

In response to my article 'Why the New Popular Poetry Makes More Sense' (*Poetry Review*, Vol 85 No 3, p46) Kennedy wrote a letter (Vol 85 No 4, p95) in which the new critical dogmatism is

admirably displayed. He suggests that John Fuller's poetry cannot be any good, is not worth considering, not for what it is, but because he represents "the exclusive, superannuated and largely discredited London–Oxbridge centre". The language of this is only a step away from "the running dogs of capitalism" style of abuse, which is where it derives from. Dare we say it: good poetry might even come from Oxford. Kennedy is a great admirer of Glyn Maxwell and wishes to see him rescued from the blokeish clutches of a Nick Hornby, and to assert his essential *difficulty*, but Maxwell is, like Auden, MacNeice, Larkin, Fuller and Fenton before him, an Oxford poet. Currently, the liveliest critics around are those writing for the new Oxford magazine *Thumbscrew*. Some superannuation; some discredit. Kennedy has obviously decided that he doesn't have to read anything that comes out of Oxford anymore because he has prior knowledge of its worthlessness. A curious attitude for a critic who was so concerned to make *The New Poetry* as *representative* as possible.

Kennedy and others litter their texts with facile references to postmodernism. But the use of postmodernism in poetry is a relatively trivial sideshow. As I understand it, postmodernism is critique of all realist philosophies. I take a realist view of the world and language as necessary for the employment of metaphor, the essential hinge between a poet's language and the material world. Shakespeare's brazen appropriations of physical imagery would not have been possible if he hadn't believed in the reality of the world. It is no accident that the postmodernist era has shown a steady weakening in the use of metaphor throughout society. So far has this gone in America that *Schindler's Ark* had to be retitled *Schindler's List* for the film because the reification of salvation in the image of the ark was deemed to be beyond the grasp of a significant proportion of the film's potential audience. In the next issue I shall expand on the metaphysical importance of metaphor for poetry.

The petulant recipes of postmodernist theorising applied to poetry are only the latest in a long line of dishonourable criticism that has dogged the century. The poetry deserves much better. For Eliot's path of difficulty was not the path taken but the path that people *imagine* was taken. MacNeice has a wonderful essay** in which he lists the stock

---

* *Post-Structuralist Readings in English Poetry*, ed. Richard Machin and Christopher Norris, CUP, 1987.
** 'The Traditional Aspect of Modern English Poetry', in *Selected Literary Criticism of Louis MacNeice*, ed. Alan Heuser, Clarendon Press, 1987.

objections to modern verse: all his examples are taken from Shakespeare. The poetry of MacNeice and Auden, despite their acknowledged debt to Eliot, brought English poetry closer to Shakespeare than it had been in the 350 years between them. There are many passages in Shakespeare that now sound Audenesque. Shakespeare may be difficult; Auden may be difficult – but not in the modernist way. The myth of modernism played into the natural laziness of much of the population. There was now a cast-iron reason for never going anywhere near new poetry. Despite the fact that English poetry hasn't really been Modernist since 1935 there is no anthology that does justice to English poetry in the twentieth-century. Edna Longley explores the twentieth-century anthologies on page 8 of this issue.

What the theorists of modernism and post-modernism have done is to encourage poetry that needs justification, critical props, excuses for the wilfulness of self-indulgent individuals – as if most needed any further excuse. But self-indulgent art will never last beyond the life of its mutual support coterie system – what lasts and what ought to matter at the time is art that has escaped all special pleading, all excuses. "Everything personal soon rots", said Yeats "unless packed in salt". As an exceptionally self-conscious century ends we can start to see what had built-in preservative and what did not. The recent tendency towards a trivial recycling of retro styles is turning into a more serious look at what will pass from this century into the next.

The process can be seen in its most fascinating form not in poetry but in popular music. The extraordinary attention focused on the Beatles'

oeuvre recently owes something to hype, but the best book about them, Ian MacDonald's *Revolution in the Head* * is a work of serious but lively criticism, and MacDonald is both open to the appeal of the Beatles and severe on their errors and delusions. Every song is analysed and the one with the widest implications is his discussion of 'Being For the Benefit of Mr Kite'. Constructed from the text of an old circus bill found by John Lennon, it is one of his best songs, but Lennon wasn't happy with it: MacDonald says: "Yet Lennon was by nature – and later by principle – distrustful of objective art (i.e. anything that didn't directly concern him). Unable to appreciate the pleasure his imagination gave to others, he fashioned things like this with fluent ease only to reject them for having none of the pain by which he measured creative authenticity". What is most luminous in the Beatles' work now are those things Lennon hated: songs about "being postmen and secretaries and writing home". 'Eleanor Rigby', 'Penny Lane' and 'She's Leaving Home' are objective art: their clarity and creaturely texture will ensure that they will always be listened to with pleasure and gratitude.

Poems should be at least as objective as good pop songs but most poets are Lennons, not McCartneys. The poet who articulated MacDonald's philosophy *avant la lettre* was of course Auden in his belief that poems should be verbal constructs. When I think of poetic equivalents of 'Penny Lane' or 'Eleanor Rigby,' it is Auden's 'The Fall of Rome' that comes to mind first.

'The Fall of Rome' works as a series of filmic images: it pans very fast across the collapse of an

---

* Ian MacDonald, *Revolution in the Head: the Beatles' records and the sixties*, Pimlico, 1995.

entire civilisation: literally Rome but by implication also our own. The images range from a close up of a bored clerk to the extremely desolate and remote image at the end, suggesting that life will go on, but in a manner incomprehensible to the fallen. You could imagine 'The Fall of Rome' written by the Beatles. Lennon would have contributed "I DO NOT LIKE MY WORK" and McCartney would have swapped "wearing her face that she keeps in a jar by the door" for "herds of reindeer move across / miles and miles of golden moss / silently and very fast".

'The Fall of Rome' is not yet a work of popular art, but 'Funeral Blues' is and its case is instructive. The lack of recognition of the real achievements of English poetry in the 20th century meant that when it was read in *Four Weddings and a Funeral*, it was almost certainly the first time millions of people had ever heard poetry like that – objective art, a verbal construct, almost 60 years after it was written. Until the film Auden was not a feature in the media, and

the critics and academics, those guardians of the flame of English literature, had always been distinctly sniffy about him. (Ian Sansom writes on Auden's critical history on page 15).

Poetry is an old art but if 'Penny Lane' and 'Eleanor Rigby' are quintessentially 20th century art then so are 'Funeral Blues' and 'The Fall of Rome'. 'Funeral Blues' could only have been written in the 20th century: it strikes a universal emotional chord but its imagery – "Pour away the ocean and sweep up the wood" – owes something to surrealism. It is a world away from Georgian lamentation. What 'Funeral Blues' proved was that given the chance to hear a fine 20th century poem in a sympathetic context, millions loved it. To date, 200,000 have bought the pamphlet of the poem. Kipling's 'If' belongs entirely to the 19th century. One day the 20th century will be seen as a golden age of English poetry. It would be good if this recognition started to dawn before the century finally checks out.

CHARLES BOYLE
A CERTAIN AGE

"At evening supper, the father is eaten up by the children".
– Louise Bourgeois

The men soldier on, treading water.
They keep leaving the garden gate unlocked.
They dream of their winning shots through the covers
for the under-16s, wake with a familiar sour taste in their mouths
that reminds them of their fathers, and in summer
they train their eyes not to linger
on their neighbours' teenage daughters' legs
by calling to mind their own.

The women cry easily.
Having forgotten what it was they wanted
they will stop suddenly in the middle of the street
causing two-mile tailbacks. Later they remember
and wonder why it seemed so urgent. On Tuesday afternoons
I accompany them in spirit
as they drive out to the gravel pits
to watch the rain.

Girls from war-torn countries who smoke in the park
are just one of our badges of guilt.
Sometimes a great wind blows in from the east
and we huddle together feeling poor and bare and forked.
Next day he's still there, like the government,
like life as it needn't be but is,
the hairy muttering man at the end of the road
clutching the noise of his own brain to his one good ear.

Tired, late, after the waiters have all gone home,
we stare into each other's eyes until one of us
is forced to look away. Truancy haunts us –
people who simply vanish, or the story of the mine-worker
who, rounding the shoulder of the mountain,
saw an avalanche had buried all his mates.
The whole landscape held its breath.
He had no second thoughts.

Bright, handsome and devouring children,
already older than we think, may be all we have.
We watch them curiously, helplessly, like exotic animals.
We teach them our bad habits.
When they go into hospital we sit outside swing doors
reading free magazines
while waiting for the nurse to come out and tell us the worst,
it's her job to do this.

No one asks us what our hobbies are, people don't
as a rule ask questions. Our secret wishes?
Our biggest mistakes? Our sorrows, consolations, distinguishing
features? When strangers to these parts
look at me twice, thinking they know me,
thinking I'm 'Roger', friends, I say, Romans, I'm a man,
I've been around if not far, I can hum a few tunes,
my patience is finite, I swing my arms as I walk.

Charles Boyle's new collection, *Pale Face*, was published by Faber in February.

Signposting the Century

EDNA LONGLEY CHARTS THE TWENTIETH CENTURY ANTHOLOGIES

"I read the sign. Which way shall I go?"
– Edward Thomas

WHILE ANTHOLOGIES SURVIVE, a notion of tradition survives. They house intricate conversations between poets and poems, between the living and the dead. In more polemical converse with one another, some anthologies dramatise the contest over aesthetic terms and values; and, as time goes by, they betray the hidden forces that also shape canons. A. Alvarez puts the matter more bitterly, when he calls "the English scene . . . savage with gang warfare which, at a distance, can be dignified as disagreements between schools of verse". Even in these days of anxious pluralism, anthologies cannot be all things to all readers. Since Linda France's *Sixty Women Poets* must omit the sixty-first, why not a bolder choice of fewer names? As Louis MacNeice said of G. S. Fraser's *Poetry Now* (1956), which includes seventy-four poets, "oh, the inevitable bittiness of it!" Edward Lucie Smith, who set out to compile "an extremely broadly based non-partisan anthology" (*British Poetry Since 1945*), confesses: "There is no avoiding the fact that making an anthology is an act of criticism". Andrew Crozier and Tim Longville deny that their introduction to *A Various Art* (1987) involves any "polemic apology or manifesto"; but to call "the poetry generally on offer" elsewhere "either provincial or parasitically metropolitan" is to advance the school of Prynne. And, like them or not, it is the most aesthetically partisan anthologies – *Des Imagistes*, Michael Roberts's *Faber Book of Modern Verse* (1936), Robert Conquest's *New Lines* (1957), Alvarez's *The New Poetry* (1962) – that have influenced the practice of poetry.

Harold Monro writes: "to each decade its poet: Centuries think in different terms". Before the millennium blows all the stars about the sky, I've been re-reading some anthologies that, with modern self-consciousness, whether in retrospect or prospect, sought to signpost the century. They include: Fraser, Roberts, Conquest and Alvarez; Monro's *Twentieth-Century Poetry* (1929), Roberts's *New Signatures* (1932), Yeats's *Oxford Book of Modern Verse* (1936); Allott's *Penguin Book of Contemporary Verse* (1950); Heath Stubbs and Wright's *Faber Book of Twentieth Century Verse* (1953); Larkin's *Oxford Book of Twentieth Century English Verse* (1973); Enright's *Oxford Book of Contemporary Verse 1945-1980* (1980); Morrison and Motion's *Penguin Book of Contemporary British Poetry* (1982); Hulse *et al's The New Poetry* (1993).

Anthologists attach poetry to history by pronouncing their enterprise epochal, contemporary, or new. Two of these categories may merge. The epochal anthology claims to speak for an age: Yeats plotting the gyres "from three years before the death of Tennyson to the present moment"; Larkin ambiguously nominating the century as his co-editor ("poets judged either by the age or by myself to be worthy of inclusion"). Contemporary anthologies are usually mid-period reckonings by mid-life anthologists whose watchword is "representative". Like epochal anthologies (and like the recently extended *Golden Treasury*) they tend to collapse in a lottery of names. Enright holds his nerve, but Allott admits to being "less and less selective as [he] approached the present", because "the sorting-out process of time" has operated less on the 1940s. Fraser and Heath-Stubbs/Wright print poets in alphabetical order, thus suppressing the role of "time" whether as critic, history, or tradition. Larkin cops out by franchising the last stretch to Anthony Thwaite's "superior knowledge of contemporary literature". How poet-anthologists engage with juniors as well as seniors says something about their own readiness for creative growth.

"New" anthologies cover the smallest time span, being future-oriented and edited by young men in a hurry (Morrison and Motion are "new" despite "contemporary" in their title). Alvarez proposed "to read the entrails and prophesy the direction poetry might soon take". Whereas "contemporary" anthologists write plangent introductions ("In terms of spectator sport . . . poetry has sunk in the hierarchy to around the level of marbles or yo-yo" – Enright), here the tone is confident, brisk, peremptory: "The poet is in some ways a leader"; "The most glaring fault waiting correction when the new period opened was the omission of the necessary intellectual component from poetry"; "What poetry needs, in brief, is a new seriousness"; "Typically, they show greater imaginative freedom and linguistic daring than the previous poetic generation"; "Every age gets the literature it deserves". Writing on English and Irish anthologies in *Irish Review* 14 (Autumn 1993), Carol Rumens notes: "Perhaps the desire to elect leaders and order everyone else to fall into step behind is a quirk peculiar to English male anthologists". (Latterday "pluralism" overcompensates for this attraction to hierarchies rather than galaxies.) Monro's anthology and *New Signatures*, separated by three years, contrast as the prematurely epochal and the impatiently new. Monro mingles "Georgians" and imagists – not always poles apart – while prophesying that "the strong influence of Mr T. S. Eliot is [most] indicative of future tendencies" up to 1940. Yet *New Signatures* already proclaims "a clear reaction against esoteric poetry" and a return to "the possibilities of counterpointed rhythm". The deep epochal swell carries cross-currents that are hard to read if one is caught up in them.

"**Margins are not *ipso facto* significant; the centre–periphery opposition cannot avoid patronage; and the only true metropolis is the shifting locus of creative and critical vitality.**"

Yet for poet or critic to trust "the sorting-out process of time" (an increasingly unstable concept) is to lose time. Superficial first impressions turn into lazy received opinion, then into academic dogma that roots like couchgrass. In *The Poetry of W. B. Yeats* (1941) MacNeice attacks "the puritanical book-reviewer who demands that any one poet should be all the time a specialist, confined to his own sphere (the reviewer allocates the sphere), and all the time self-consistent". And when, for instance, a poet like Keith Douglas falls between anthologies (he is not in Allott), the art becomes damagingly ignorant of itself. Douglas understood how the true shock of the new challenges readers and writers: "Poetry is like a man, whom thinking you know all his movements and appearance you will presently come upon in such a posture that for a moment you can hardly believe it a position of the limbs you know". *The Faber Book of Modern Verse* may owe its long influence to a unique blend of the epochal and the new.

Young poets edit anthologies to secure their future, older poets to secure their posterity. Even the genial *Rattle Bag*, edited by Ted Hughes and Seamus Heaney, conceals some such motive behind the naturalising claim that it "amassed itself like a cairn". Yeats and Larkin notoriously try to pass on their literary genes; in part, through poems that they misread as made in their own image. Thus Yeats favours pseudo-heroism from Oliver St. John Gogarty, Larkin pseudo-ordinariness from Betjeman and other versifiers. Beyond overweening individual shadows, however, we glimpse real aesthetic controversy in which national and generational tensions are implicated.

How twentieth-century anthologists construe / construct relations between "English", American and Irish poetry is my main focus. Has this historical struggle for metropolitan authority no bearing on the devolutionary and multicultural models of today? To quote Hulse *et al.*: "[X's] circumstances as a black Briton adopted and raised by a white Scottish family may be taken as an extreme example of what Terry Eagleton has termed 'the marginal becoming central'". That sentence can hardly be taken as an example of an aesthetic proposition. Nor can Crozier and Longville's confounding of province and metropolis in the name of some higher authority (Cambridge?). Neil Astley is on surer ground when he says in *Poetry with an Edge* (1993 edn): "Bloodaxe has been accused of an anti-metropolitan bias [but] this 'provincial' publisher is actually more national and international in outlook than its London counterparts". Margins are not *ipso facto* significant; the centre–periphery opposition cannot avoid patronage; and the only true metropolis is the shifting locus of creative and critical vitality.

But what is Bloodaxe's nation? Alternatively, what has the national anthology to do with poetics? A glance at anthologies of Irish poetry would disclose warfare which few editors "dignify as disagreements between schools of verse". Here clan as well as coterie is at stake. Similarly, anthologies of Scottish poetry plait its linguistic strands gingerly in the context of an emergent cultural nationalism. Roderick Watson introduces *The Poetry of Scotland: Gaelic, Scots and English* (1995) with the cry

"Anthologists beware", and continues: "The only agenda-free anthology of Scottish poetry would be a project worthy of Borges's notion of the universal library". National or regional anthologies inevitably propose to "sustain, imply, construct or seek a version of ourselves" (Watson). Lacking this dimension, poetry would deny its communal origins. But what such anthologies gain in cultural definition, they lose in aesthetic precision (which cultural definition needs) and the ramifying affiliations it introduces. For years London provided the most vigorous critical forum in these islands. As a refuge from local commissars it was – up to a point – excused its south-eastern bias and unconscious English nationalism. London magazines and publishers gave English-language poetry some freedom of circulation. Today, with the unarticulated English question on the literary as well as cultural agenda, and with morbid symptoms of hegemonic anxiety appearing, it may be useful to ponder the dynamics of a rich period when British, American and Irish poetry were peculiarly intimate.

Yeats's *Oxford Book* became notorious in Ireland for excluding Austin Clarke, in England for excluding Wilfred Owen, and in America for excluding Americans – except two poets "of long residence in Europe". Babette Deutsch wondered "why HD does not fit into this category". Yeats distances America as Larkin uses Thwaite to distance the young: "A distinguished American poet urged me not to attempt a representative selection of American poetry; he pointed out that I could not hope to acquire the necessary knowledge". Yet the triple offence given by Yeats was strategic as well as mischievous. On the "national" front Irish poets did well (bad personal relations with Yeats explain Clarke's exclusion). Stephen Spender called the anthology "that Irish fen dominated by twin giants Lady Dorothy Wellesley and Mr W. J. Turner". In *Left Review* Cecil Day Lewis, perhaps included for Ireland, bemoaned for England:

> The omission of the war poets, together with the inadequate representation of some of the post-war writers – notably Auden and Spender – detracts very seriously from the value of Mr Yeats's anthology. A reader of fifty years hence, . . . would receive an erroneous idea of what has happened in English poetry. The extracts from Eliot and MacNeice would give him the impression of a disintegrating age hardening into fragmentary fatalism.

Day Lewis then praises some execrable communist verse from *The Year's Poetry 1936*. Yeats's line on the trench poets may actually have less to do with "passive suffering" (his own poetry assimilated the war) than with restoring his battered Irish nationalist credibility. As for "what has happened in English poetry" since 1930: although the skimpy selection from Auden puts down the young (English) pretender, Yeats's finale is more open to difference than Larkin's.

Indeed, he recruits Auden, MacNeice, Spender and Day Lewis for Ireland against America; or, more specifically, against the rival genes of T. S. Eliot, who "produc[ed] his effects by a rejection of all rhythms and metaphors used by the more popular romantics rather than the discovery of his own". Yeats heralds the new poets by saying: "in this mood of sympathy I prefer them to Eliot, to myself – I, too, have tried to be modern". And he crucially binds their techniques – "handl[ing] the traditional metres with new freedom – *vers libre* lost much of its vogue some five years ago" – to his own. He gets left-wing politics out of the way by calling the poets' intensity of belief "not political", and by reading Auden's "lunar beauty" as Yeatsian transcendence. Yet, *pace* Day Lewis, he may have identified deeper tendencies of the "disintegrating age". Meanwhile, back in Ireland, Austin Clarke thought that Yeats had betrayed the Literary Revival, opted for Anglo-Irishness, and sold out to England. MacNeice would later describe Yeats as impatient with his posterity in Ireland, and as leaning towards "English poets who were breaking his own rules". Here MacNeice uses the *Oxford Book* to declare forms of Anglo-Irishness central to the Yeatsian succession.

In the *Faber Book of Modern Verse* the new generation inhabits the different context created by starting with Hopkins rather than with Pater, and by Roberts's American horizons: not only Pound and Eliot, but Aiken, HD, Moore, Stevens, Ransom, Tate, Crane, Cummings. In fact, Roberts includes good selections from Owen, Rosenberg and Graves, and distinguishes between "European" (mostly expatriate American) and "English" poetry on the basis that the former depends more on literature and "existing cultural values", the latter on "first order . . . intensification of qualities inherent in the English language itself". Perhaps this obliquely reclaims ownership of the language from across the Atlantic. Yeats is placed in both camps. Roberts excludes some poets, such as de la Mare and Muir, who "have written good poems without having been compelled to make any notable development of poetic technique". For him, development in technique is tied in with negotiating psychological, political or philosophical "crisis". He starts with "The Wreck of the Deutschland" because "working in subterranean fashion [Hopkins] moulded a style which expressed the tension and disorder that he found inside himself". Yet Roberts's review of techniques is not biased towards modernist effects, and he knows that poetry eludes the critic's categories. What eludes his own categories, however, is how disorder and technical development might be found in Hardy and Edward Thomas.

Between them, Conquest and Alvarez upset the *Faber Book's* English-European or, rather, Anglo-American balance. Conquest's opening sentences make no bones about the politics of anthologies:

> In the late 1920s a group of poets were starting to write who were to be the typical poets of the 1930s. Towards the end of the 1930s a group of writers with quite different attitudes began to emerge, who were to dominate the 1940s. Each of these groups was, if not launched, at least presented to public fire by anthologies which took up definite positions.

Such tactical relegation of poets still on the job drew fire from MacNeice: "This game of pigeon-holing literary generations has gone too far . . . Posterity may find our generations closer to each other than we care to think". But, bent upon domination, Conquest exaggerates difference by caricaturing the 30s and 40s: "great systems of theoretical constructs . . . agglomerations of unconscious commands". This refusal of politics and psychology gives hostages to political and psychic subtexts. On the aesthetic surface Conquest makes a plea for "intellect", for "a rational structure and comprehensible language, even when the verse is most highly charged with sensuous or emotional intent". However, one subtext may be English centrality: "lallans-mongers", as well as the supposedly Celtic Dylan Thomas (important to Larkin and Wain), are sidelined. Another subtext may be the war. Whereas 1930s writers admitted their irrational guilt about missing the test of 1914–18, Alvarez is surely right to notice repression, cultural confusion and aesthetic hiatus here. Among its other qualities, poetry in the 1940s was structurally influenced by diverse war-

zones. Conquest proclaims Orwell's "honesty" exemplary, without reference to its contexts. Similarly, he does traditional forms some service – singling out Graves, playing Yeats for England against American modernism as "the great poet of the century" – except where he implies that forms and meanings can invariably be controlled. This Augustanism denies dimensions that have accrued to all poetry, not only modernist poetry, in the twentieth century. The Movement aesthetic, as theorised by Conquest, is more a matter of control and authority united as "lucidity" (still a key term for Enright) than "gentility". It is ironical that his Larkin selection should begin with "Maiden Name", a poem hardly in control of its Id.

Larkin was interested in the link between two "primitive" phenomena: "poetry and sovereignty". His *Oxford Book* attempts to retrieve an English national line, most successfully in its installation of Hardy alongside Yeats – the poles of his own Anglo-Irish dialectic – and Eliot. It's strange that he does not make more of Edward Thomas, but gives him the same space as de la Mare, Gibson (who "*never wrote a good poem in his life*"), Hodgson and Masefield. This dissipates what might come from the collision between so-called Georgians and the Great War, as does too little from Owen and

Rosenberg, nothing from Sorley. Paradoxically, 1950s repression ensures that Larkin allows Eliot and Pound to swamp, as usual, the poets who underwent the crisis of English lyric and became so important in the 1930s. Neither war disturbs the anthology as Alvarez would desire: "the forces of disintegration [evil, libido] . . . destroy the old standards of civilisation. Their public faces are those of two world wars, of the concentration camps, of genocide . . ."

Alvarez nominates American leaders (Lowell, Berryman) to supply the deficiency. How does his diagnosis of an English "negative feedback" look now? He lists successive symptoms – anti-modernism, anti-intellectualism, refusal of psycho-analytical insights – which culminate in the 1950s. The first feedback depends on where you put Yeats, who, as we have seen, wanders all over the anthological map. It also depends on how you regard the renewed formalism of the 1930s, surely the period during which Eliot's impact on this side of the Atlantic was definitively sifted. This is one reason why the *Faber Book* wears so well. Secondly, intellect or intelligence in poetry is not the same thing as the poet being an intellectual, even if increased dependence on academe further blurs the distinction. Although I am sympathetic to Alvarez's third point, he may require the unconscious as conscious theme (Hughes) rather than as protean actor ("*natural* fouled-up guys"). Yet Alvarez was right even when he was wrong, even when, as he admits, his anthology does not bear out its "inflammatory introduction". He was right in linking poetry's scope and ambition to a sense of being challenged by its own history. English neomodernism and post-modernism, however, are often unhistorical. In different ways, Michael Horovitz's *Children of Albion* and Crozier and Longville's *A Various Art* use timeless American modernism as a stick to beat contemporary poetry. The former's anarchism, the latter's academicism, take single elements of the modernist matrix to extremes of Left and Right. "A street urchin rolling in moss" versus the pedagogic tone of "Poetry was seen as an art in relation to its own conventions – and a pusillanimous set of conventions at that". Paladin's *The New British Poetry* (1988) makes strange bedfellows of this old-style "alternative" ("the poetics of modernism") and a new-style stress on "Black British Poetry" and poetry by women. The politics of English anthologies evidently reflect the ideological dynamics of English politics in general.

Unhistorical in another way is Hulse *et al's The New Poetry* ("Eighties Britain grieved observers"). Relentlessly "now", it lacks Alvarez's epochal awareness. Indeed, it unwittingly pronounces the death of tradition: "the beginning of the end of British poetry's tribal divisions and isolation, and a new cohesiveness – its constituent parts "talk" to one another readily, eloquently and freely while preserving their unique identities". This individualistic chat-line model evinces a familiar confusion. How relations between poems constitute tradition differs from how relations between people constitute society. Earlier, D. J. Enright argued that "the best movement is one that doesn't move far in the same direction". But mutual awareness need not mean mimicry – the diversity of Northern Irish poetry suggests the contrary. Did his solipsistic vigil benefit Larkin in the long run? Carol Rumens contrasts the collectivities she finds in anthologies of Irish poetry (despite their raw disputes) with the "carefree rootlessness" of *The Penguin Anthology of Contemporary British Poetry*". While saluting Seamus Heaney as their Ulster general, "Motion and Morrison do not delve far into the roots of the Irish flowering, nor search out the historical points of confluence between Irish and English poetry that underwrite the current exchanges". Many points of confluence – Anglo-Welsh and Scots-English as well as those I have discussed – created "modern" poetry, whether it begins with Pater or Hopkins or Hardy or Homer.

Here are a few conclusions: (1) war poetry should not be half-delegated to specialist anthologies; (2) aesthetic conviction, as opposed to something else masquerading as aesthetics, keeps an anthology alive; (3) poets who die prematurely may be forgotten when the epochal, the contemporary and the new are constructed – men of letters hang in there for ever; (4) what Roberts calls "the false poem" obscures the true; (5) English poetry may honour an occasional Irish master, but it has generally grovelled to America; (6) partial and polemical versions of the 1930s and 1940s have eroded a historical sense of the modern movement; (7) there is no consensus as to Auden's most significant poems: perhaps muddle begins at his crossroads in 1939; (8) mechanisms of tradition are ultimately impersonal: a point that English Wordsworthianism recurrently forgets; (9) not to remember the past is to be condemned to write the same poem over and over again.

DAVID GASCOYNE
ONCE MORE

These poems, all dating from 1936, were recently retrieved from notebooks by the author.

Goût du Jour

Today there is fur on the tongue of the wakening light
There is dust in the darkening streets
Whose tongue is brick dissolved in lime
The sound of sight
Reduced to ashes by the height of the bloom's decay
In the caverns of the smell
Where moth-balls leap like mole-hills in the pocket of grey fowls
Thin grey fowls with leather gullets
And with claws of too much rain
Too much anthracite in pain
In the cities of the plain
Although anthrax is the secret of the way to find your way
From the paling of the pillars to the breaking of the bars
Where the breezy bellows stand in bright array
And the castanets are forming little holes in women's sleeves
In order to allow their sound to breathe.

Cafard

Sickness and charity like death's heads tied to the mast
Return to the bottomless sea from whence they came
Where islands of snow sink like holes into the heart
And the revenge of death is remembered no more
By those whom the firmament betrayed
Life's nebulous champagne is forgotten before it is drunk
For each of its bubbles is a brief lapse of its blood
Of the somnolent clay whose arms embrace the sleeper
And whose veins are of lead – life's bouquet
Has lost all its scent for those who plucked it
Their senses are tied to the battlecry's torn floating web
And the landscape's oblivious light is
Where islands of snow sink like holes into the heart.

Recuperation

The gradual emergence of the
Instincts the hard sharp
Laughter of the sudden daylight
And out of the sleepy funnel
Of the waking mouth
Breath
Merges again with the waiting
Whiteness of what is to be.

PETER WYLES

SINGING OUR SONG

It is cold in the castle, and once again
there are warming pans in the royal bed,
too big a bed to sleep in alone.
She's still in the tower, working to rule,
singing our song but humming the words
she was happy to say out loud when we met.
I don't care. I'm still the King
and I won't have the dwarves in the place again,
pawing my son, and staring at my wife,
muttering dwarvish things in their beards.
People will talk. Well, damn the lot of them,
the half-made men in their bachelor pad
hidden in the woods at the edge of my kingdom.
I just don't trust them – their spaniel eyes
and their sullen looks when I take her hand.
There should be a law against half-made things,
and empty beds, and humming the words.
People are questioning my choice of Queen.
They were happy enough to cheer at the time.
I won't have them saying its my eye wandering –
it has all gone wrong, and I don't know why.
Those dwarves aren't natural. Why does she want them
to brush her hair, and to teach my son
God knows what wild and dwarvish things?
I've given her everything. I've done my duty,
she's as good as locked herself into the tower.
People must be talking behind my back.
There should be a law called Happy Ever After.
Her Prince did come, and his castle's cold.

What's Become of Wystan?

AUDEN'S REPUTATION SEEMS UNASSAILABLE BUT IT WASN'T ALWAYS THE CASE.
IAN SANSOM LOOKS AT HIS CRITICAL HISTORY.

THE JURY SEEMS finally to have come to a verdict, but not without argument along the way. "He was useless", protested MacDiarmid, "a complete wash-out". "No he wasn't", countered Brodsky, "he was the greatest mind of the twentieth century". "Come on", said John Whitworth, "he was good, but not that good". "He was a complete professional", replied Glyn Maxwell. "A professional?" echoed the voice of Leavis from beyond the grave, "He was a poetaster, immature, inadequate . . ." "Hey, leave it, Leavis, the guy was cool", threatened a group of New Yorkers and a couple of ageing Beats. "I liked his early stuff", offered a bald guy at the back wearing bicycle clips. "Oh, shut up Larkin", said the Americans. "Shame!" cried the Brits.

During the 1930s W. H. Auden was widely regarded by critics and by his contemporaries as the saviour of English poetry, a kind of superman, an *Übermensch*, a poet of unique insights and abilities: "Auden does not fit. Auden is no gentleman. Auden does not write, or exist, by any of the codes, by the Bloomsbury rules, by the Hampstead rules, by the Oxford, the Cambridge, or the Russell Square rules", enthused Geoffrey Grigson in the 1937 *New Verse* Auden Double Number. Frederic Prokosch described Auden's talents as "immense"; Dylan Thomas described him as "wide and deep"; in the 1933 *New Country* anthology Charles Madge trembled with excitement at the thought of Auden and his poetry:

But there waited for me in the summer morning,
Auden, fiercely. I read, shuddered and knew.
And all the world's stationary things
In silence moved to take up new positions.

And Cecil Day Lewis in the same book ejaculated, "Look west, Wystan, lone flyer, birdman, my

> "During the 1930s W. H. Auden was widely regarded by critics and contemporaries as the saviour of English poetry, a kind of superman, an *Übermensch*, a poet of unique insights and abilities."

bully boy!" Even MacDiarmid, in his great polemical autobiographical prose work *Lucky Poet* (1943), attempting to define "The Kind of Poetry I Want" had to devote much of his time to defining "the kind of poetry I don't want", i.e. "the Auden-Spender-MacNeice school". Whether you liked it or not, Auden was a force to be reckoned with.

His move to America in 1939 put an immediate end to the hype and the adulation and condemned him to the uncertain status of expatriate. Many writers and critics simply never forgave him for leaving. On reading of Auden's death Anthony Powell was rendered speechless with joy and disgust: "I'm *delighted* that *shit* has gone . . . It should have happened years ago . . . scuttling off to America in 1939 with his boyfriend like a . . . like a . . ." Auden, it was felt, had deserted the nation at its hour of need.

Yet it was probably not the fact of his leaving England on the eve of war so much as the sheer fact of war itself that caused the widespread change of opinion about Auden's work. Cyril Connolly, discussing the work of Auden, Spender, Isherwood, Day Lewis and MacNeice in 1943 argued that "The output of these five people was, in fact, not a literary movement, but a heavy industry. What put an end to it? The answer is in one word, Hitler". G. S. Fraser claimed that it was in fact Dunkirk that proved the death of the "Auden manner": "It was impossible, after Dunkirk, to feel that our national tradition was as rotten as the poets of the 1930s . . . had made out. Somehow, unexpectedly, we had pulled ourselves together; even from the point of view of 'social awareness', a certain reaction against the Auden manner was called for". Auden, quite simply, was out of date.

He reinvented himself in America, which the English resented. He didn't actually take the oath of allegiance and become an American citizen until 1946, but by then he had long been accepted into the American literary establishment. Reflecting on the poetry scene in America in the 1940s, Randall Jarrell, Marianne Moore and Robert Penn Warren all put it bluntly: "Auden is the only poet who has been very influential recently"; "W. H. Auden's influence on American work is very marked, and general"; "it is certainly true that Auden, especially, has had great influence on the younger American poets". The Americans responded warmly to his pomp and his frivolity and respected his ambition.

Back in England, Leavis inaugurated a period of revaluation of Auden's work with the 1950 "Retrospect" to his notorious 1932 *New Bearings in English Poetry*. In the retrospect Leavis stumbled through an explanation of why he had not included Auden in his original account, grudgingly admitting that Auden had "made a rapid advance in sophistication" but quickly dismissing sophistication as belonging "to a climate in which the natural appetite for kudos is not chastened by contact with mature standards". An even more devastating attack came ten years later, in 1960, with Larkin's review of *Homage To Clio*, despairingly but affectionately titled 'What's Become of Wystan?' in which Larkin set out a strong case against the later Auden: bookish, superficial, "too verbose to be memorable and too intellectual to be moving". The tone of disappointment and sceptical disenchantment was picked up by the trend-spotting *Penguin Guide to English Literature* in 1961, which announced, "It is Auden's most sympathetic interpreters today whom we find doubting, even after the fullest possible survey of his poetic range and quality, whether he can be claimed as a major artist".

The standard view, then, was that Auden was finished: his work unserious, his reputation declining. According to John Fletcher, writing in *The Spectator* in 1969, "Auden, who has known vogue in the past, seems to be a rather unfashionable poet these days. The earnest young don't appear to have much time for his wry kind of introspection". But the critics, not for the first time, had got it wrong. The earnest young had in fact rather a lot of time for Auden. They were busy appearing on stage with him, for example, at the Poetry International festivals in London, and Allen Ginsberg even made a pilgrimage to Ischia especially to visit him (when Ginsberg visited Auden in Oxford in 1958, he

attempted to kiss the hem of his trousers; Auden was not amused). In 'Prologue at Sixty', the last poem in his 1969 collection *City Without Walls* Auden asked, "Can Sixty make sense to Sixteen-Plus?" The answer, apparently, was yes.

After his death in 1973, after the inevitable rush of tributes, there was a lull of interest in Auden's work. Writing in *Poetry Review* in 1978 Sean O'Brien stated categorically that "Auden's paradoxical imagination . . . has not had much effect on postwar English poets". But three years later he detected a new "common ground" in the Audenesque in the work of Tom Paulin, Douglas Dunn and Paul Muldoon, and in 1994 he claimed that "Auden's influence on his successors is so large and so various as to make him part of the poetic weather". So what had happened between 1978 and 1994 to make O'Brien change his tune? What had happened to regenerate Auden's influence and reinflate his reputation among critics and readers?

An obvious answer is the film *Four Weddings and a Funeral*, the 1994 box-office hit in which Auden's poem 'Funeral Blues' was read as an oration at the funeral of a gay character, played by Simon Callow. Faber rushed out a pamphlet of ten of Auden's poems, titled *Tell Me the Truth About Love*, to cash in on the film's success and Random House, Auden's American publishers, produced an 'audiobook' of the same title. There were reports of sales of over 200,000 copies of the pamphlet, and Faber even decided to produce a long-awaited paperback edition of the *Collected Poems*. Some commentators were cynical about such profiteering, but on this occasion the cynicism missed the point; the poetry had struck a chord, as James Fenton explained in an article in *The Independent*: "It seems that a large number of people, since the Aids epidemic, have become familiar with the experience of funerals at which a devastated boyfriend has to pay tribute to his prematurely dead lover. Though the death of the Callow character is actually caused by a heart attack, the emotional scene that ensues gains force from those kinds of memories". Auden's, it seems, was a poetry whose time had come (again).

Certainly, during the 1980s, in a Britain restless under the rule of an uncaring Tory government, the example of the political engagement of the poets of the 30s had a certain appeal. Auden's political stance has in fact been variously regarded as an example to be followed or a mistake to be avoided;

as the critic Frederick Grubb argues, Auden "remains central to literary discussion" partly because he "doubles the parts of scapegoat and avatar in our sub-conscious. We envy, to the point of nostalgia, the poet who enjoyed a social stimulus; we imagine how much more efficient as heroes and revolutionaries we might have been". If in the 1930s he was generally regarded as a leftist (though in fact his political activism amounted to little more than driving a car in the General Strike, his abortive trip to Spain and a spell with the left-leaning GPO film unit), and in the 1950s praised and condemned as a romantic and a liberal, so in the 1970s, 80s and 90s writers have found him to be engaged and disengaged according to taste: "When Auden said his poetry didn't save one Jew from the gas chamber, he'd said it all", Tom Stoppard told one interviewer; "*Letters from Iceland* offers a response to history, politics and society which is not only still valid, but which has still to be followed", claimed Tom Paulin. Glyn Maxwell, in an essay published in 1994, went so far as to proclaim that Auden could provide an alternative to the sterile British two-party political system:

> In a country that has been psychologically vandalised – I would say traumatised, perhaps irredeemably – for fourteen years, by the kind of thinking that says there is only One Way, only One Truth, only One Right Way to think – Auden's work stands as an enduring monument to difference, compassion, the multiplicity of truth and the morality of the various . . . I dream that a political opposition might group itself not around the sense that its own truth is the One Truth, but about that multiplicity, that belief

in manifold nature, that morality of the imagination that I believe is best exemplified in Auden's work.

President Auden is perhaps not too hard to imagine.

Whatever the reasons, in responding to various crises and dilemmas over the past twenty years writers and critics have entered into a new dialogue with Auden's work, and in particular seem to have rediscovere what the critic Barbara Everett once called Auden's "sense of the askew, of inhabiting a moment that gains definition only from the degree to which it lacks the absolute" (surely as good a definition of the postmodern as any). This is certainly borne out by the editors of the controversial *The New Poetry*, which claimed to represent "the best poetry written in the British Isles in the 1980s and early 1990s by a distinctive new generation of poets", who argued that the new poetry was "above all *sceptical*" and that its "defining presences are, consequently, most often to be found in John Ashbery, W. H. Auden, Elizabeth Bishop and Derek Mahon" (Ashbery, Auden and Bishop, yes, but Mahon?). In his review of *The New Poetry* Peter Porter enthused that "At last the legacy of W. H. Auden has begun to bear fruit in his native land". The jury, then, has found in his favour; the critics, for the moment, have been silenced. There are rumours, however, that the prosecution is preparing an appeal . . .

Ian Sansom teaches at Brunel University College and reviews for the *London Review of Books*, *The Guardian* and *Thumbscrew*.

THE CLASSIC POEM

1. SELECTED BY CAROL RUMENS

When I was young, I read Louis MacNeice as an Englishman and Oxonian – marvellously clever and fluent, a shade frightening. (Auden's equally clever voice sounded friendlier.) It was not till I got to Belfast that I learned to read MacNeice as an Irish poet. This understanding turned perplexed admiration into love. The poem is No. III from 'Flowers in the Interval'. Terza rima is notoriously hard to do well in English. MacNeice does it effortlessly: he sings it, with a great forward-rolling surge of energy, and floods of glorious, slightly self-mocking but passionate imagery. I wish I had written it. I wish I had someone to have written it to.

Carol Rumens' latest collection, *Best China Sky* (Bloodaxe), will be reviewed in the next issue.

LOUIS MACNEICE
FROM: FLOWERS IN THE INTERVAL

Because you intoxicate like all the drinks
We have drunk together from Achill Island to Athens,
Retsina or Nostrano, pops and clinks

Through snow or mist or mistral, aquavit
Or Château Neuf du Pape, from coloured inks
To the blood of bulls or sun-gods, dry or sweet,

Bitter or mild, armagnac, ouzo, stout,
Because, like each of these, you reprieve, repeat
Whether dry or sweet your newness, with or without

Water, and each one ray of you distils
A benediction and an end to doubt
Because your presence is all rays and rills;

Because your presence is baths of freesias, because
Your eyes are the gold-flecked loughs of Irish hills
Your hands are Parvati and Millamant and what was

The earliest corn-and-fire dance is your hair,
Your stance is a caryatid's who seems to pause
Before she slips off, blandly unaware

Of the architrave on her head, because your moods
Are sun and water and because the air
Is burnished by you and the multitudes

Of humble moments answer to your voice
Like goldfish to a bell or sleeping woods
To a fresh breeze, because you make no choice

Unless you feel it first, because your laugh
Is Catherine wheels and dolphins, because Rejoice
Is etched upon your eyes, because the chaff

Of dead wit flies before you and the froth
Of false convention with it, because you are half
Night and half day, both woven in one cloth,

Because your colours are onyx and cantaloupe,
Wet seaweed, lizard, lilac, tiger-moth
And olive groves and beech-woods, because you scoop

The sun up in your hands, because your form
Is bevelled hills which neither crane nor stoop,
Because your voice is carved of jade yet warm

And always is itself and always new,
A pocket of calm air amidst a storm
And yet a ripple beneath all calms, a view

Into wide space which still is near; is you.

Reprinted by permission of David Higham Associates from Louis MacNeice,
Collected Poems (Faber & Faber).

Faber have recently reissued several MacNeice titles: MacNeice's autobiography,
The Strings are False (see p79), Edna Longley's *Louis MacNeice: A Critical Study*
(£7.99, ISBN 0 571 13748 2); Jon Stallworthy's biography, *Louis MacNeice*
(£12.99, ISBN 0 571 17687 9).

2 . SELECTED BY PETER PORTER

Can a translation be a modern classic especially if it is of an ancient classic? It can when it is as consummate as this of one of Horace's fine Odes. Louis MacNeice taught classics in Birmingham when that city was a centre for Auden as well. His version of Horace was probably written for radio. In the *Collected Poems* it is dated 1936–38, and was first published in the volume *The Earth Compels*. He also translated two other odes, including the celebrated 'Carpe Diem'. The third, fourth and fifth stanzas also turn up , in slightly different wording and unacknowledged, in Auden's BBC radio feature *Hadrian's Wall*, which marks the first appearance of 'Roman Wall Blues'. Included as well is the early Latin hymn 'Jam lucis orto sidere', again later translated by MacNeice and which in its plainchant form provides the cantus of Benjamin Britten's church parable *The Prodigal Son*. Britten wrote the music for *Hadrian's Wall* and subsequently for MacNeice's Group Theatre play *Out of the Picture*, his radio feature *The Dark Tower*, and also made a setting of 'Cradle Song for Eleanor' for Hedli Anderson, MacNeice's second wife. Perhaps this immaculate rendering of Horace was in Auden's mind when he and Kallman wrote the book for Henze's *The Bassarids*. Whatever its affiliations, MacNeice's poem catches the sensuality, raciness, and melancholy of Horace as no other translation has ever done for me.

Peter Porter's latest collection is *Millennial Fables* (OUP).

THE ODES OF HORACE
BOOK 1, NO. 4, 'SOLVITUR ACRIS HIEMS . . .'

Winter to Spring: the west wind melts the frozen rancour,
    The windlass drags to sea the thirsty hull;
Byre is no longer welcome to beast or fire to ploughman,
    The field removes the frost-cap from his skull.

Venus of Cythera leads the dances under the hanging
    Moon and the linked line of Nymphs and Graces
Beat the ground with measured feet while the busy Fire-God
    Stokes his red-hot mills in volcanic places.

Now is the time to twine the spruce and shining head with myrtle,
    Now with flowers escape the earthly fetter,
And sacrifice to the woodland god in shady copses
    A lamb or a kid, whichever he likes better.

Equally heavy is the heel of white-faced Death on the pauper's
    Shack and the towers of kings, and O my dear
The little sum of life forbids the ravelling of lengthy
    Hopes. Night and the fabled dead are near

And the narrow house of nothing, past whose lintel
    You will meet no wine like this, no boy to admire
Like Lycidas, who today makes all young men a furnace
    And whom tomorrow girls will find a fire.

TRANSLATION BY LOUIS MACNEICE

Reprinted by permission of David Higham Associates from Louis MacNeice, *Collected Poems* (Faber & Faber).

A SECOND LOOK

Stroking This Stone

P. J. KAVANAGH ON GEOFFREY GRIGSON'S
'SECULAR HEAVEN ON THIS EARTH'

THERE WAS NO writer quite like Geoffrey Grigson in the decades between 1950 and 1980. None more various – poet, autobiographer, botanist, rediscoverer of Samuel Palmer, propagandist for Ben Nicholson and Henry Moore – and none more useful.

In earlier decades (he was born in 1905) he had been celebrated for his literary feuds, in his own magazine *New Verse*, and elsewhere. The violence of these can still astonish. In the Notes to his anthology *Before the Romantics* (l946) – he was, far from incidentally, the greatest anthologist of his time: *Before the Romantics*, *The Romantics*, and *The Victorians* are acts of creative criticism, showing what he liked and saying why – even in his entertaining Notes, he can slash out with what he called his "billhook" as though attacking weeds, which he felt he was doing: literary overgrowths. Defending seventeenth-century Nathaniel Lee, ". . . there is plenty as ridiculous, and not as clearly written and attractive, in the present-day Welsh gut-spinning school, in some of Miss Edith Sitwell's gilded sprawlings, and in the poems of almost any number of *Penguin New Writing*". This is the sound of a man hacking, alone, at what was most fashionable, most conventionally praised in his time; it makes you sit up. Grigson came to regret these muscular swings, to feel they were energy wasted, but he hardly repented. Musing, towards the end of his life in *Recollections* (1984), he wonders if it is true that Betjeman "climbed from his house at Uffington and cursed me, from the backside of the White Horse? Why not? John Betjeman showed himself a kind and forgiving man, but I detested and still detest his verses, or most of them". To Grigson, the modernist, Betjeman's poems sounded like sops to the complacencies of the middle-class, in technique were pastiches or parodies of the rhythms of *Hymns Ancient and Modern*. Impatient Grigson

was not the sort of man to put up with, or see through, the defensive mask of giggling snobbishness that Betjeman sometimes affected. The snobs could hit back – "Grigson's the sort one asks in for coffee *after* dinner" Cyril Connolly is reported to have said, but one can imagine Connolly falling on Grigson's neck in apology, and Grigson remaining obdurate, stiffnecked. Unlike Anglo-Irish people (or Anglo-Dutch people) Grigson seems consciously to have abjured charm, as though putting such oil into the social machine was a hypocritical emollient, *grease*. This constitutes (it would annoy him to hear) the source of his attraction.

He was almost an exotic in his English-rootedness, with the national characteristic of being bloody-minded. Though he disliked Philistine bluffness and quotes with approval Manley Hopkins's verdict on Browning, that he sounded too often like a man with a mouthful of bread and cheese declaring he would put up with no more of this damned nonsense, Grigson could sometimes sound like that himself, almost. Only "almost", because he is saved by the honesty of his grasping at the Here-and-Now, with no bombast or faking, and with no blurred edges to suggest that it meant anything but itself. With what coltish nervousness he avoids, checks at, rears up neighing (naying) before the transcendental.

His need to write poems sanitised of the spiritual presented him with several difficulties. How, observing grace, beauty, and being moved by these, to avoid the metaphysical? Since his emotion derived chiefly from natural forms, how not to sound like his detested Georgians, or the poets of the *London Mercury* c. 1930, whom he knew to be candidates for the billhook? How not to appear, Heaven help us (a plea he would be unlikely to make), a country-sentimentalist in well-cut tweeds; or worse, like the Sitwells? His answers to these questions are what give his writing, especially his poetry, its bumpy vitality.

He was, he said, "no religionist". Perhaps, after all, his dislike of Betjeman was directed at his "churchiness". Grigson was the last of seven sons of a country parson, and always believed that inside every poet is a perfect place, a perfect time, to which he returns; a touchstone, whether consciously so or not. His "heaven" was his boyhood in his father's Cornish parish. He writes of it in *The Crest on the Silver* (1950). It was a flawed paradise, of course, because of his nature, loneliness, imperfect relations with his parents (especially his mother), varied feelings towards his brothers, one of whom, at least, he hated. He discovered early that he did not believe in his father's God but in Consciousness, in the Moment. "What else but Now is deity, / And worth adoring?" Too easy to assume this is a reaction; it goes deeper, is more important: a poetic. Instructive that *The Crest on the Silver*, the account of a boy enchanted by a defined pocket of Cornish landscape, its woods, hedges, pools, flowers, insects, fish, succeeds memorably for its first two-thirds, but as it approaches his present self becomes a disjointed series of jottings. In this case a mistake; but a foreshadowing of his method as a poet. He set himself to learn how to catch the present moment without falsifying; or rather, to re-learn how to catch it. In midlife he understood that he had lost his boyhood wonder, and he wanted it back. "I had to force myself to *look*, to look at even the simplest things, and then perhaps the simplest things could involve themselves with the complex, stripped of association, the statement shut within the experience and the enjoyment of the senses". He called it "a discipline of abandonment". But he never quite abandoned his indignations. "There remained the occasional temptation towards the billhook". Yes, far too late in his *Collected Poems 1963–80*, Betjeman again toddles into Grigson's view:

> If wearing my old goat's skin down Reviewer's Lane
> I cried the birth of a Byron or a Blake again,
> Who would look out, or even hear,
> Or give up buggering his bald teddy-bear?

This is pointless, when around venomous spurts like that one the billhook is being wielded in a more useful and original fashion: keeping God (the vague) at bay, admiring a momentary pattern of clouds; but, of course,

> By this is excused nothing,
> Illuminated nothing, symbolised
> Nothing – unless accident, accident . . .

Sometimes he abandons impressionism to make his intention explicit:

> When out at night
> I wish to express my wonder
> Seeing a whole moon through white
> Clouds in a great ring of amber
>
> Past high leaves shining
> Of a scented poplar,
> God, I say, My God,
> What a bloody wonder.
>
> I don't claim God in that exclaiming
> Has atavistic merit:
> It is a shell of a word
> I happen to inherit.
>
> Clumsily to that riding orb should
> I exclaim "All men who've been?"
> Well, if I take to bits My God,
> It is that I mean.

– A reasonable definition of his deity. He thinks of an early Italian painting:

> Angels, protrude your long thin trumpets glistening
> Out far from your black shelf of cloud.
> Greet, angels, with tender voluntaries of your perfection
> The minute soul flying through vast freedom
>   upwards,
> Having left behind its sagged body in a shroud.
>
> O if this could be so, I exclaim.
> But to perfection
> Have we imagined it. In such perfectness have
> As well fresh trees against light, in light
> Been painted. So much must be allowed.

For the humanist, art is its own justification. However, whereas the Christianity which Grigson cannot accept contains crucifixion as well as redemption, Grigson's problem is to show that his epicureanism includes an awareness of Hell: that his celebration of the senses, adoration of Now, requires an effort on our part and on his, is *in despite of*, as the contorted syntax suggests. He frequently insists, "I say", meaning "*nevertheless*, I say", to suggest full acknowledgement of circumambient terror; but "I say" we must still enjoy, look, smell, touch:

> Knowing home was, knowing there is no going home,
> Knowing there is no home;
> Yet stroking this mottled, sometimes as now sun-
> heated,
> By the water shaped and polished stone.
> Stroking this stone.

He spells it out in *Blessings, Kicks and Curses* (1982), a collection of late essays. After a supperful of horrors on television news: "I am saying in brief to hell with more hell in our minds than is justified. I am saying we should do better with rather more recognition, rather more celebration, of secular heaven on earth when it does briefly and on that account poignantly occur". That is from 'Poems and Pleasure' in which he comes close to conceding that painting can better express his intention. "In the Tate there is a picture quivering with enjoyment in exactly the way I mean, in the simplest terms and by the subtlest devices – go and look at it – Sisley's *Path to the Old Ferry*".

How characteristic is "quivering", and that "go and look at it"; and how useful.

P. J. Kavanagh's *Collected Poems* were recently reissued by Carcanet in paperback.

Bibliography

The British Library database has 34 books by Geoffrey Grigson, most of which are no longer in print (those which are in print are indicated here by an asterisk). The others, which include books of poems, anthologies, art and literary criticism, reminiscences and English topography, are all worth searching out.

Before the Romantics, an anthology of the Enlightenment, Salamander Press, 1984.
Blessings, Kicks and Curses, a critical collection, Alison & Busby, 1982.
Britain Observed, the landscape through artists' eyes, Phaidon, 1975.
Collected Poems, Alison & Busby, 1982.
The Englishman's Flora, Phoenix House, 1987.
The Faber Book of Poems and Places, 1980.
The Faber Book of Epigrams and Epigraphs, 1977.
**The Faber Book of Love Poems*, 1983.
**The Oxford Book of Satirical Verse*, 1983.
Persephone's Flowers (poems), Secker & Warburg, 1986.
The private art, a poetry notebook, Alison & Busby, 1982.
Recollections, mainly of writers and artists, Chatto & Windus, 1984.
**The Shell Country Alphabet*, Michael Joseph, 1966.

NEW POETS '96

EACH ISSUE THIS YEAR WILL FEATURE TWO OR THREE POETS
WHO HAVE YET TO PUBLISH A FULL COLLECTION

ATAR HADARI

BORN IN ISRAEL and raised in England, a verse playwright and poet, he was
first published in the *Times Literary Supplement* at twenty when shortlisted
in the 1986 Poetry Competition. He won a scholarship to study with Derek
Walcott at Boston University where he wrote and staged his play *Possessions*,
a retelling of Anski's *The Dybbuk* which went on to gain him a playwrit-
ing Fellowship at the West Coast's premier theatre, the Mark Taper Forum.
Back East his one-act play *The Woman and the Woods* drew praise in the Love
Creek One Act Festival and a production on New York's 42nd Street, later
revived at London's Canal Cafe Theatre. His translations of the Hebrew national poet Bialik are
collected in a volume, *Songs from Bialik*, to be published this autumn by Syracuse University Press.
His poems have appeared in Britain and the US in magazines such as the *American Poetry Review,
Poetry East, Poetry London Newsletter, The Wide Skirt,* and the *Jewish Quarterly,* where he contributes
a column on writers and performers. Currently he is the first ever Munroe Moore Fellow chosen to
be Playwright in Residence at the Fine Arts Work Center in Provincetown, one of America's oldest art
colonies, where he has completed plays about Alexander Pope, Janis Joplin and others. Three influential books: *Complete Poems and Plays* of T. S. Eliot, *Collected Poems* of Philip Larkin and *Complete
Poems* of Thomas Hardy.

INCIDENT IN THE CAFE,
HUNGRY GENERATIONS

Out of the halls of men she goes
old, bitter, unsteady of hand and clothes
stick in her hand, the tricky zip
on the red woollen cardigan just sticks
and sticks for five long minutes while
the boy just by her table waits and smiles
and does not say he waits but stares
for her shadow out of the front door
and her back to all of the glamour
music, cup clangs, saucers, chatter
as he takes her coffee table
and she walks into the leaf-fall
blind to all but light that in the gutter still burns.

ANOTHER DUCHESS

That's my last Duchess passing in the hall,
sounding as if she had a world to call
her own, other than mine, in which she breathes
at least, while I'm inclined, these days to wheeze
whenever I hear female tread go past;
and every time the cough subsides
I see her painted on the inner wall
of my eye and have to scrub the balls
of my palms on my brows, till I hear fall
of her foot or at least another who can drive
the famished feast of her face from the curve
of every tray, replacing it with a starvation dish
of someone pleasant, pleasant is the very least
I'll be content with – but they're not her.
Sorry, sorry – really, let's not bother
talking anymore about her, are you
comfy there on that side? There, I'll throw
my pillow in there for you, there, how's that?
Neck better? Just a minute to put out
this fag. We have all night. The dawn won't come
while we're still in a sweat. Relax. The gleam
on the windowsill reminds me of her teeth.
I'm sorry – can you get my wallet out from underneath
the jacket? . . .What d'you mean why not just talk?
She isn't somebody you'd simply walk
up to in the park, make a remark
apropos of the mating ducks, oh how they clear
the water with their white wings, would she eat dinner?
That night, any other night? Maybe? I want her
more than ducks pawing at water want the air
but I can't get clear of her, into flight. Shan't
be mentioning it again. Pass me the water
and another rubber. Look, the light. I wonder
if she's cold now, or holding someone or other?

THE NEWS STAND

She sits facing the wall of bodies
buttocks, thighs, upreared hearts bustiered to
explode as soon as the coin fingering thumb lifts,
drops the change and walks out to
sunlight and the riffle of endless paper hearts ease.
She sits in the shaded counter
newsprint wafts across her face
like flies on a dying baby's forehead
she stares at the breasts but doesn't see
light – yellow, stacks of envelopes, glue, whistles
poised with a pea silenced inside their throat
magazines with advertisements for sailboats
blue water like the veins straining out of her hands.
She smells. It must be said.
A foot away, two feet, some food
or laxative, or soap powder
reeks off her like petrol fumes.
She slumps facing the doll face
facing her out of the racks
one huge white and porcelain
face waiting to descend on hers
with no opening for mouth.
And she stills, watching the spider
idle across her palm toward the glue
she can't open the mask mouth
only the teeth in all those lipstick mouths
will one day have to come
and tear her cheeks apart.

TESSA ROSE CHESTER

I WAS BORN IN 1950 and grew up in North London. Drawing and writing poems and stories from an early age, I was eventually steered towards a career in illustration and began a Foundation course at Harrow Art College in 1968. I left the course abruptly on my marriage and moved to Cambridge, where my three children were born. I put together a couple of exhibitions there in the 1970s but have done little drawing since.

When my first marriage ended I worked for two years at Cambridge Central Library before doing a four year honours degree course in Librarianship at the Polytechnic of North London. For the past fourteen years I've been Curator of Children's Books at Bethnal Green Museum of Childhood in London. For ten years I read and wrote no poetry at all owing to the pressures of my job and daily commuting from Cambridge, where I still live. However, I was writing reviews, articles and books in connection with my work.

Nineteen ninety, my fortieth year (during which I became a grandmother), seemed an appropriate point at which to start being creative again. It took a while to get to grips with the contemporary poetry scene, but gradually my poems gained acceptance in magazines such as *Staple* and *The Rialto*. In 1994 I won joint first prize in the Blue Nose Poets of the Year competition, and came third at Bridport, and now Oxford University Press are bringing out my first collection, *Provisions of Light*, in November. 'The Minden Sonnets' were written as a kind of homage to the beauty of one particular place and to the people concerned who lent me that space without question. Here, perhaps, are the bones of an answer.

THE MINDEN SONNETS

1.

If it's a question of leaving, just go.
Bludgeoned by silly words, that nagging need.
When blood is roused by every verbal blow

and we allow each other to misread
our actions. When we will not, cannot stop;
when we kill anything that moves. Go, feed

the cat, pack bags, go. Let others prop
the family up. Cut loose, take slow ways down
to catch the season's smell, the smoky drops

of rain, the aromatic breath of towns.
Primeval longing speaks from other years
but I hesitate, almost turning round.

Sehnsucht pulls my understanding clear.
To want something this much; to be this near.

2.

To want something this much; to be this near,
trying to summon precious texts by name.
Drawn compulsively from Chichester

to Pevensey through earth-bound links, chains
of church and castle, Iron Age hill-fort,
chorused like a children's singing-game:

Cissbury Ring, Devil's Dyke, Ditchling, Firle. Taut
bronze beacons whirl above the flowery hush
of villages. Flint-and-brick wall the court-

house, cottage, school, while ancient beech and brush
mask the mythical Green Man lying low.
Ask a boy the way to Birling Gap. Crush

shingle in your hand, snuff the air, follow
the confluence of water and the crow.

3.

The confluence of water and the crow.
The ghosts of shepherds on the South Downs Way,
counting-out from Went Hill to Haven Brow.

The succulence of limpet-pie, bouquet
of periwinkles from the farm. Shell
and gull in every field. The slow decay

along the coast, fragile darkness of Belle
Tout, Seven Sisters in their blood-stained shifts
crumbling passively under the swell

of moons and tides. Go where dunlin drift
among fleshy sea-plants, glasswort, aster;
the salt-marsh estuary, where redshank sift

for worms in muddy creeks. Pallid Cuckmere,
river of the calligraphic signature.

4.

River of the calligraphic signature,
vast shining loop of pastoral elegance
etching marsh and meadow: its allure

inducing a controlled hypnotic trance
round Alfriston. June: the cloudy Tye
billows cotton-wool; summer brilliance

clarifies the white wood bridge, Plonk Barn's flight
of snowy doves, geese in a protective fan.
Through golden wheat to Lullington; close by,

the chalky footpath to the giant Long Man
of Wilmington. Up on Windover Hill
there is unburdening. Test your wingspan

for the coming age! Stretch out all sense, feel
the earth's muscles flexing our free-will.

5.

The earth's muscles flexing. Our free-will
discharged by rhythms from historic hours:
tremor of rock, stammer of stone; fibril

energies, minute pulsating showers
barely registered. Invisibles we
refuse to name, yet which contain such power.

To rest; down to Litlington for tea.
Meditate on autumn's weeping bruise
beneath the cawing monkey-puzzle tree.

Clap cups; shake rain; chase yesterday's news
rusting away in amber leaves. Mature
here slowly, meld with umber shadows, lose

your conscious self on purpose to ensure
tranquillity becomes a ligature.

6.

Tranquillity becomes a ligature
of dreams I am reluctant to dispel;
far better this than having to endure

fictive realities. Something propels
me on to reach the house, deep and calm
among the hills, a Sleeper, immortelle,

cupped in the Downs' accommodating palm.
A place of gatherings; not quite an end
nor yet a start. A garden like a psalm

to ease transition. Here I can depend
on anonymity, cast off the chill
of being who I am. A place to mend

all those uncertainties, re-learn the rules
of resolution, ways of being still.

7.

Of resolution, ways of being still.
Having lost our grip, mislaid the crib-sheet
for our lives, we are unmanageable,

dancing in the internecine streets.
*We'll survive if we stay mobile; plot
and counter-plot will save us from defeat.*

Now we have forgotten how to stop.
This house runs tutorials in slowing
down; it organises polyglot

diplomas, seminars in knowing
when it's time to pause, to mitigate
the temper of the present. Owing

that much to self I should co-operate,
bound to a place in which I can relate.

8.

Bound to a place in which I can relate;
stringing word-palaces from room to room.
Listening. Syllables reverberate;

through the air they oscillate in perfumed
nuances. I seize them when I can,
pin them quivering to the page, assume

my role as butcher, baker, artisan
for – how long will it take? – here in this house
of curious brightness, where the pale light scans

my face as I write or sit and browse;
where morning comes white as limpid crystal
on my skin, engraved like glass as I drowse,

with feather, beak and claw. Where I reveal
anticipation of the possible.

9.

Anticipation of the possible
unfurls like a sleepy cat. The air thrums,
membrane-marked by imperceptible

incisions from jagged wings that come
and go across the cerulean sky.
Birds zing like shuttles on elastic looms;

with constant busyness and poignant cry
they soak the house in contrapuntal song
and measured madrigal. They prophesy

eternal winters, crippling rain, long
periods of drought. They celebrate
rich harvests in uneven carillon.

We peck in stippled shadows, and debate
each negative examined, isolate.

10.

Each negative examined, isolate.
This pack of guilt; that box of bulldozed
argument; parings of neglect; the weight

of rotting errors, sent to decompose
beyond the shrubbery, out of sight
of present circumstance. Enough to close

the gate and walk into the melting light
of scorching summer days; to watch the wren
rouse the buddleia, the teazels ringed bright

with goldfinches, the twilight bustle when
blackbird and thrush descend to entertain
their young around the pond. Enough to blend

into the shallows with unravelled pain,
to wash away misfortune's chequered stain.

11.

To wash away misfortune's chequered stain
that charges lives with sharp anxiety;
to challenge thought with no thought, yet remain

receptive, open to the rarity
that one's unconscious little gods provide
through an increased suggestibility.

The garden's many voices speak aside;
an echo from the Song of Solomon.
Shuddering blue waves of the dignified

Cryptomeria; the Rose of Sharon's
starry yellow shawl; apples, spices; great
clumps of spurge; basil, thyme and tarragon;

mauve spotted orchids, wild and delicate,
encourage all that's natural, innate.

12.

Encourage all that's natural, innate.
A kiln of bees with a generator
hum possess the house; I concentrate

on opening windows, slowly crossing floors.
Microscopic movements catch my eye
under the moon – froglets, ghosting raw

transparencies of veins, their struck surprise
quickening the grass. The house clears its throat.
At night I cannot sleep: you occupy

each room, your warmth and erudition quote
the principles of living under strain.
Absorbing traces of your remote

love, I wear you like an inner skin;
small breakages become composed again.

13.

Small breakages become composed again:
the sorry face domestic business wears,
the sad confusion of the mind's campaign.

Our set addiction to material cares;
the power dependence builds; our silent part
as witness to the TV film that dares

record destruction while we wait. The art
of camouflage, of false despair; our trick
of stepping to one side while staring out

the century. Collective doubt, the thick
pall of shame we never quite explain.
All this, dissolving in a neutral flick

of time, allowing discontent to wane.
Small acts of wounding heal in your domain.

14.

Small acts of wounding heal in your domain
as time becomes ephemeral. I cling
to what I know, and walk about the lanes

as though reprieved. Ordinary things
and deeds conceal the real significants
of life. Symbols of security in

everyday disguise, they imbibe our chance,
our suffering, with casual concern;
their textured mouths form compelling entrance

to the past; memory by touch. I turn
a page; this writing has your voice. I grow
into your coat, your chair, and keep Minden

with me, after, like a kind of charm. So:
if it's a question of leaving, just go.

15.

If it's a question of leaving, just go.
To want something this much: to be this near
the confluence of water and the crow,

river of the calligraphic signature,
the earth's muscles flexing. Our free-will,
tranquillity, becomes a ligature

of resolution, ways of being still.
Bound to a place in which I can relate
anticipation of the possible,

each negative examined, isolate;
to wash away misfortune's chequered stain,
encourage all that's natural, innate.

Small breakages become composed again.
Small acts of wounding heal in your domain.

IN APPRECIATION OF

Joseph Brodsky 1940–1996

JOSEPH BRODSKY, WHO DIED IN NEW YORK ON JANUARY 28TH AT THE AGE OF 55, WAS
A POET FOR WHOM ELEGY WAS OF SUPREME IMPORTANCE. WE PRINT TRIBUTES FROM
TWO POETS AND EXTRACTS FROM JOSEPH'S OWN TRIBUTE TO STEPHEN SPENDER.

Anthony Hecht

I can think of no other poet, in any language or any period, who was as ruthlessly and grandly enmeshed in the inhuman, transcendent ironies of history as was Joseph Brodsky. His enormous griefs and joys, his survival and his demise took place on an international stage. Branded by his countrymen a "semiliterate parasite whose pornographic and anti-Soviet poetry would corrupt the young", he was sentenced to five years of internal exile at heavy labor of the most demeaning and exhausting kind; but so great and widespread was the protest from distinguished Russians like Akhmatova and Shostakovich that he was released after eighteen months of chopping wood and shovelling shit, and other brutalities of a punitive schedule he described in a Commencement Address at Williams College in 1984; and was sent into exile. The blessings of this freedom, the gifts of a better life, were secured at the cost of separation from the parents he adored, the language and landscape that meant most to him, and the permanent severance from his young son, Andrei, as well as all the friends he had ever known. He settled in a country that had hardly heard of him, and was generally indifferent to his lonely plight.

In due course his poetry, translated first by others but later by himself (for he continued to compose in his native tongue, and to turn his work into English only later), as well as his prose essays and literary appreciations brought him to the notice of a warmly admiring world-wide audience and the Swedish Academy. But at a cost: he underwent two by-pass operations and was scheduled for a third at the time of his death. Shrewdly suspecting he might die on the operating table, he was trying to postpone that surgery until he had completed his teaching duties for the spring term at Mt. Holyoke. But against all warnings from

physicians and friends, he went on smoking, and was a helpless, terminal addict. When literary recognition finally came it was accompanied by a blissful marriage to a beautiful and intelligent woman, Maria Sozzani (half Russian, half Italian) and the arrival of a daughter, Anna, probably named in homage to Akhmatova. But this blessing was of the briefest duration, cut short as it was by his premature death at the age of fifty-five.

You might suppose that a *vita* such as his – which, before he was brought to trial and sentenced had included work as a milling-machine operator, helper in a morgue, photographer (his father's profession) and participant in geological expeditions – would supply any poet with the materials for a life-time of writing. But Joseph Brodsky wrote about himself in only the most circumspect way, shunning self-dramatisation as something unseemly. Though history played grotesque tricks on him, it never ceased, in its overpowering, impersonal force, to enthral him: one of his poems is called 'Letters from the Ming Dynasty', and another 'Twenty Sonnets to Mary Queen of Scots'. His poems, ranging the whole surface of the earth and the vast annals of civilisation, were at home everywhere, since everywhere is the domain of the exile, including galactic reaches as well as terrestrial topography, the space-time continuum and the unalterable laws of physics. Cheated as he was of formal education after the equivalent of our ninth grade, he taught himself English, Polish, German, Italian and French, and made himself acquainted with all the world's greatest poets, living and dead. But Clio, with her wry smile, was his unfailing Muse. He shares his gifts for irony with History itself, and with perhaps a few other poets, Hardy and Cavafy among them; but not one of them has ever matched his supremely sardonic, amused, resigned and cheerful eloquence. With something like prophetic vision he traced, in a magnificent poem called 'A Hawk's Cry in Autumn', the astonishing trajectory of his own brilliant career.

Two posthumous books, one of poetry, one of prose, are scheduled for publication in the near future. And there is no reason to expect any diminution in the excellence or range of his work. Other writers have been tamed or daunted by the

award of the Nobel Prize, but not this man, whose talents and imaginative life seemed boundless. Almost everyone who knew him was aware that, intertwined with his genius was an extraordinary integrity that made him an uncommonly good man. Within a year of his winning the Nobel Prize he had given much of that bequest away to writers whose needs he regarded as greater than his own. We shall not look upon his like again.

Gwyneth Lewis

I had the great good fortune to be one of Joseph Brodsky's students at the Writing Division of Columbia University in New York in 1983. I was present to hear his now famous analysis of W. H. Auden's 'September 1, 1939' (reproduced in his selection of essays, *Less Than One*). When I read that poem now I always hear it with Brodsky's heavy Russian accent, modulated by a slangy American intonation, an unforgettable mixture. The moment he started talking in the first seminar I attended, I was utterly captivated by his total commitment to poetry as a force. He was the first person I'd ever met to whom poetry was a life-or-death matter. I had always *felt* this to be the case, but after I knew him and attended his classes, I knew *why* it was so. If, as Auden wrote, time worships language then metre, Brodsky argued, was, in itself, reconstructed time. In my notebook of that year I wrote that he told us that "the movement from speech to poetry is the fullest possible evolutionary development for man in his life – that is, you have to get as good as you can". His passion about this made us renew our own, even though the stakes seemed almost paralysingly high for a young poet.

Each week he made us learn a great poem off by heart – Hardy's 'The Convergence of the Twain' and 'Channel Firing', Frost's 'Acquainted with the Night' and 'Neither Out Far Nor in Deep'. I'm ashamed to say that I used to rebel against this stricture and deliberately arrive late to avoid the written memory test he set at the beginning of each seminar. Of course, I now regret it. He taught us Hardy, Frost, Auden, Cavafy and Holan. I have lived off these classes for ten years or more and continue to do so.

Joseph's intelligence was breathtaking. He showed me that a poet could think about and contribute to the whole scope of a culture's argu-

ment with itself – be that in politics, science or history. He was clear about the moral temptations of writing (immorality is always clothed in a bad style, he said) and about the vulnerabilities of the poet, who hears those who mock his raptures even as he writes. He alleged that you could always tell the difference between an European and an American poem by the third line, because of their different metrical agendas. In writing an essay, he said, you should always finish it and cut out the opening paragraph (he was right, I did it to this tribute).

In his classes, Joseph made no concession to ignorance, laziness or lack of total seriousness about poetry. He was rightly intolerant of the common American ignorance or hostility towards the metrical disciplines. This could make him seem harsh, but it was always done in the interest of poetry. He was always kind to us individually. He came to dinner (I cooked bluefish and rice) and we talked feverishly about poetry all night. My friends and I were so excited by his conversation, ranging from his memories of Anna Akhmatova to the invention of the zip, that after he left we went out to see the Thanksgiving Parade balloons being inflated in Central Park. I got mugged on the way home, which seemed a fittingly dramatic end to an unforgettable evening.

We met for lunch occasionally. One time I broached the subject of the difficulty I was having in deciding in which language – Welsh or English – to write. "I envy you the English language", he sighed, and talked rapturously about his late love affair with it (or should I say her?). He hadn't pontificated (which he was perfectly capable of doing) but had drawn my attention to the value of a tradition which I was taking for granted. I saw that what I had was an opportunity, not a problem. He opened my eyes another time by asking how I was earning a living. I said I wasn't really. "Ah", he said with great feeling, "the garret is vastly over-rated as a place to work", words which helped me see that a regular income could be an aid to writing, rather than a distraction from it; this improved my standard of living no end.

Another time when we met I was very depressed and homesick and when he was sympathetic I started to cry. "There, there, Gwyn", he said, "you should go to the Mediterranean, find a hotel room and look at the far distant line of the sea". Fortunately I had the sense to see that this was the last thing I needed, but the advice was kindly meant and was obviously *his* recourse in times of emotional disorientation. He felt his exile from Russia keenly, especially when he was unable to see his parents again before their deaths.

As his students, we were always worried about Joseph's recklessness with his health. He continued to chainsmoke, despite having serious heart problems. He would bite out filters with savage impatience. He attended classes wearing a hospital bracelet during one especially difficult period with his heart. This fearlessness, however, was the logical conclusion of his poetics. It came out of his aesthetic conviction that failing his duty as a poet was more to be feared than anything life or the Soviet authorities could throw at him. The poet's only duty was to avoid the temptations which would weaken his work and thus consign him to oblivion.

Joseph had a wonderful combination of utter respect for tradition and an avidity for modern American life. He would wheel out the most preposterous jokes – I remember one particularly awful one about the assassination of Rajiv Gandhi. Execrable puns gave him particular delight. He was totally unafraid of bad taste, a great strength in a poet because it precludes the self-censorship which cuts out both the worst and the best portions of inspiration.

To his students he showed the importance of working to the highest possible standards in poetry: his life showed us the cost and the joy of doing so. Like W. B. Yeats, he has become his admirers. Our gratitude to him means that that admiration will be lasting. There is one last footnote. Joseph died on January 28th, the same day as Yeats. He had just delivered a manuscript to his publishers. In the timing of his death he slipped even closer to W. H. Auden's poem to Yeats which he loved so much, whose lines may stand as a monument to him:

> Follow poet, follow right
> To the bottom of the night,
> With your unconstraining voice
> Still persuade us to rejoice;
> . . .
> In the deserts of the heart
> Let the healing fountain start,
> In the prison of his days
> Teach the free man how to praise.

From: In Memory of Stephen Spender

by Joseph Brodsky

IF YOU ARE born in Russia, nostalgia for an alternative genesis is inevitable. The Thirties were close enough, as I was born in 1940. What made the decade even more congenial was its grimy, monochrome denomination, owing chiefly to the printed word and black-and-white cinema: my native realm was of the same shade and stayed that way long after the Kodak invasion. MacNeice, Auden, and Spender – I mention them in the order I found them – made me feel at home at once. It wasn't their moral vision, since my enemy, I

believe, was more formidable and ubiquitous than theirs; it was their poetics. It unshackled me: above all, metrically and stanzaically. After 'Bagpipe Music', the good old tetrametric, quatrain-bound job seemed – initially at least – less tempting. The other thing I found terribly attractive was their common knack for taking a bewildering look at the familiar. Call this influence; I'll call it affinity. Roughly from the age of twenty-eight on, I regarded them as my relatives rather than as masters or "imaginary friends". They were my mental family – far more so than anybody among my own contemporaries, inside or outside of Russia. Chalk this up to my immaturity or to disguised stylistic conservatism. Or else simply to vanity: to some puerile desire to be judged under a foreign code of conscience. On the other hand, consider the possibility that what they did could be loved from afar. Or that reading poets writing in a foreign tongue bespeaks one's appetite for worship. Stranger things have happened: you've seen the churches.

I lived happily in that mental family. The wall-thick English-Russian dictionary was in fact a door, or should I say a window, since it was often foggy and staring through it required some concentration. This paid off particularly well because it was poetry, for in a poem every line is a choice. You can tell a lot about a man by his choice of an epithet. I thought MacNeice chaotic, musical, self-indulgent, and imagined him moody and reticent. I thought Auden brilliant, resolute, profoundly tragic, and witty; I imagined him quirky and gruff. I thought Spender more lyrical and ambitious with his imagery than both, though rather conspicuously modernist, but I couldn't picture him at all.

Reading, like loving, is a one-way street, and all that was going on unbeknownst to any of them. So when I ended up that summer in the West, I was a total stranger indeed. (I didn't know, for instance, that MacNeice had already been dead for five years). Less so perhaps to Wystan, since he wrote the introduction to my Selected and must have realized that my 'In Memory of T. S. Eliot' is based on his 'In Memory of W. B. Yeats'. But certainly to Stephen and Natasha, no matter what Akhmatova could possibly have told them. Neither then or in the course of the subsequent twenty-three years did I talk to him about his poems or vice-versa. The same goes for his *World Within World, The Thirties and After, Love-Hate Relations, Journals.* Initially I suppose the culprit was my timidity saddled with my Elizabethan vocabulary and shaky grammar. Eventually, it would be his or my Transatlantic fatigue, public places, people around, or matters more absorbing to us than our own writings. Such as politics or press scandals, or Wystan. Somehow from the threshold it was assumed that we had more in common than not, the way it is in a family.

* * *

I see the past tense creeping in, and I wonder whether I should really fight it. He died on July 16th, today is August 5th. Still, I can't think of him summarily. Whatever I may say about him will be provisional or one-sided. Definitions are always reductive, and his ability to escape them at the age of eight-six is not surprising, even though I caught up with only a quarter of it. Somehow it's easier to question one's own presence than to believe he's gone.

This is because gentleness and civility are most lasting. And his are of the most durable kind, borne as they were by the grimy, cruel, either/or era. To say the least, his manner of deportment – in verse as in life – appears to have been a matter of choice as much as temperament. In sissy times – like these – one, a writer especially, can afford to be brutal, lean, mean, etc. In fact, in sissy times one practically has to peddle gore and garbage, for otherwise one won't sell. With Hitler and Stalin around, one goes the other way . . . Ah, all this paperback brutal talent! So numerous and so unnecessary, and so awash in money. That alone can make you feel nostalgic for the Thirties and play havoc with your affinities. In the final analysis, though, what matters in life as well as on paper, with deeds as well as with epithets – is what helps you to retain your dignity, and gentleness and civility do. For that reason alone he is, and will remain, palpable. More and more so, as days go by.

* * *

And now the last fragment. A diary entry, really. For July 20th to 21st, 1995. Done, I suppose, in imitation of Stephen's journals – for I don't keep a diary.

Awfully hot night, worse than NY. D. (family friend) picks me up, and 45 minutes later we are at Loudon Rd. Ah, how well I know this place's two floors and basement! Natasha's first words: "Of all people, he was unlikeliest to die". I can't think of what the last four days were like for her, of what this night is going to be like. It's all in her eyes. The same goes for Matthew and Lizzie. Barry (Lizzie's husband) produces whiskey and treats my glass generously. No one is in good shape. Of all things we are talking about Yugoslavia. I couldn't eat on the plane and still can't. More whiskey, then, and more Yugoslavia, and by now it's midnight for them. Matthew and Lizzie suggest that I stay either in Stephen's study or in Lizzie and Barry's attic. But M. booked a hotel for me, and they drive me there: it's a few blocks away.

In the morning D. drives us all to St. Mary of Paddington. On account of my Russianness, Natasha arranges for me to see Stephen in an open coffin. He looks severe and settled for whatever it is ahead. I kiss him on his brow, saying, "Thank you for everything. Say hello to Wystan and my parents. Farewell". I remember his legs, in the hospital, protruding from the gown: bruised with burst blood vessels – exactly like my father's, who was older than Stephen by six years. No, it's not because I wasn't present at his death that I flew to London. Though that could be as good a reason as any. No, not because of that. Actually, after seeing Stephen in the open coffin, I feel much calmer. Presumably this custom has something to do with its therapeutic effect. This strikes me as a Wystan-like thought. He would be here if he could. So it might just as well be me. Even if I can't provide Natasha and the children with any comfort, I can be a distraction. Now Matthew screws the bolts into the coffin lid. He fights tears, but they are winning. One can't help him; nor do I think one should. This is a son's job.

People begin to arrive for the service and stand outside in little groups. I recognise Valerie Eliot, and after some initial awkwardness we talk. She tells me this story: the day her husband died, the BBC broadcast a tribute to him read over the wireless by Auden. "He was absolutely the right man", she says. "Still, I was somewhat surprised by his promptness". A little later, she says, he comes to London, calls on her, and tells her that when the BBC learned that Eliot was gravely ill, they telephoned and asked him to record an obituary. Wystan said that he refused to speak about T. S. Eliot in the past tense while he was alive. In that case, said the BBC, we'll go to somebody else. "So I had to grit my teeth and do it", said Auden. "And for that I beg your forgiveness".

Joseph Brodsky

Then the service begins. It is as beautiful as an affair of this kind can be. The window behind the altar gives onto a wonderfully sunlit churchyard. Haydn and Schubert. Except that, as the quartet goes into a crescendo, I see in the side window a lift with construction workers climbing to the umpteenth floor of the adjacent high-rise. This strikes me as the kind of thing Stephen himself would notice and later remark about. And throughout the service, totally inappropriate lines from Wystan's poem about Mozart keep running through my mind:

How seemly then to celebrate the birth
Of one who didn't do harm to our poor earth,
Created masterpieces by the dozen,
Indulges in toilet humor with his cousin
And had a pauper funeral in the rain –
The like of whom we'll never meet again.

So, after all, he is here: not as a comfort, but as a distraction. And out of habit. I suppose his lines used to visit Stephen's mind quite frequently, and Stephen's his. Now in either case they will be homesick forever.

The service over, all adjourn to Loudon Road for drinks in the garden. The sun is hard-hitting, the sky is a solid blue slate. General chatter; the most frequent openings are "The end of an era" and "What a perfect day". The whole thing looks more like a garden party than anything. Perhaps this is the way the English keep their real sentiments in check, though some faces betray confusion. Lady R. says hello and makes some remark to the effect that at all funerals one thinks inevitably of one's own, didn't I think? I say no, and when she professes disbelief, explain to her that in our line of work one learns to narrow the focus by writing elegies. That, I add, rubs off on one's attitudes in reality. "I meant that one implicitly wishes to last as long as the person who's just died", maneuvers Lady R. I buy the implication and move toward the exit. As I step outside, I run into a just-arriving couple. The man is about my age and looks vaguely familiar (somebody in publishing). We greet each other and he says, "The end of an era". No, I want to say to him. Not the end of an era. Of a life. Which was longer and better than either yours or mine. But instead I just muster a broad, cheerful, Stephen-like grin and say "I don't think so", and walk away.

Reprinted by permission of Farrar Strauss & Giroux Inc and Hamish Hamilton Ltd from Joseph Brodsky, *On Grief and Reason*.

Norman MacCaig 1910–1996

by Iain Crichton Smith

NORMAN MACCAIG WHO died on the 23rd January will be a great loss to Scottish poetry though perhaps in his last years he was not writing a great deal. His death however evoked even among the general public an interest which recalled that of Hugh MacDiarmid of whom MacCaig himself noted that that event should evoke two minutes pandemonium.

Part of this public affection had to do with the fact that over a long lifetime he had done many poetry readings (wittily delivered); that his work was on the syllabus of schools and universities; and that in TV interviews he came across as humorous and independent-minded, though sometimes acerbic.

As for his career, he took a classics degree at Edinburgh University and during the war was a conscientious objector which may have slowed down his promotion in the primary sector of education in Edinburgh. In his later life he was a wonderfully popular lecturer at Stirling University: he had a great rapport with the young who would not find any hypocrisy in him and who of course were delighted by his wit. He was however the least academic of poets. In his years of major creativity he would be found in Milne's Bar and the Abbotsford in the company of Hugh MacDiarmid and Sydney Goodsir Smith, a Falstaffian rumbustious poet of extrovert humour. MacCaig's wit was more excised, sometimes scathing, and with the same unexpectedness as his best poems have.

He was for many years a living link with Hugh MacDiarmid who was a close friend. Though it was not in MacCaig's nature to be sloppily fulsome about that giant figure, he had the greatest admiration for MacDiarmid who would say to him that he laid an egg every four years: Macdiarmid himself was more wastefully volcanic.

Knowing his own limitations exactly, and keeping to them, he didn't write long poems. He described his poems in terms of the number of cigarettes he took to write them. He would feel like writing a poem, at the time not having a subject in his head, then the words would begin, as he said himself, to

"trickle" down the page. He would have no truck wth White Goddesses and he valued clarity. He disowned his first two books because of their metaphoric turmoil and would tell the story of the friend who asked for answers to them. He had a wonderful sense of the music of a poem: and indeed he was a devotee of music, from Mozart to Gaelic songs.

He did not speak Gaelic though his mother was from Scalpay in Harris but he loved its great poetry and songs. In some ways the colour and exactness of his own poetry has something Gaelic about them. His presentation of Nature in exquisite accuracy and clarity is very Gaelic. His exactness of imaginative description such as in "a hen stares at nothing with one eye, then picks it up" is unparalleled.

He did philosophise in some of his poems but the best ones are purely descriptive. He did think much about the observer and the observed and the function of metaphor. He saw the world in a unique way and this issued in a special kind of poem recognisably MacCaig. His metaphorising had no effort in it; this was the way he thought. His conversational wit and the wit of his poems were all of a piece. He would talk of entries "blackening" his diary. Metaphor was instinctive to him.

He has left a great legacy of lyric poems, many of them about Nature but some about love in a metaphysical style. He was helpful to the young and admired by them. He was generous with himself and his possessions but there was also a private wariness about him. He put his trust in poetry and was repaid for it. He didn't write much criticism or do much reviewing but when he did he was notably generous. He didn't like writing prose and thought poetry far superior. I think that like MacDiarmid he didn't much read novels.

He will be remembered as one of Scotland's true gifted life-affirming writers who showed us the world in its imaginative radiant bloom. Also, unlike some poets, he was in himself and quite apart from his poetry a man of immense wit and carefully hidden erudition.

DAVID CONSTANTINE
BOMBSCARE

But we have bombscares. There was one this spring
The day before my birthday. I went in wanting
The OS map of another island
And sniffed the hush, the hush and a change in the air,
The two together: spring come and a bombscare.

A plastic tape was run all around the centre
Slight and symbolic as a sabbath wire
And nobody transgressed. The sentries
Had nothing much to do, but everyone expelled
From making a living in the centre idled

In shirt sleeves and blouses on the first day warm enough
With those kept out. You feel let off
Idling on the outside if you have to. Inside
It's like a site two thousand years from now
Uncovered clean. A police car like a UFO,

The blue light twirling. You feel absolved
More still when word comes out the thing was shelved
Among the goods a year ago at least.
The thought of it lying where you often came and went,
Its time not yet, is like a present

Coming from where you could not know one might. The tape
Ran to the shop but let me in. Sat on the step
In the sort of respite Sunday mornings used to make
Or overnight deep snow. Sat in the sun
And opened the map of another island there and then.

On the empty blue it floats like an elm-seed.
Seems mostly rock. The thin yellow road,
Run from a steamer route on the east coast,
Includes some tumuli, a standing stone or two,
A ruined oratory in the noose of its lasso.

Fifty tomorrow. From off the west coast
Peninsulars push out. The one pushing the farthest,
I fix on that. Sweet, sitting in the sun
While a man with nifty fingers whose job it is,
Breathing quietly, makes a timebomb harmless.

PETER ARMSTRONG
FROM THE VIRTUAL TERRACES

It will be late some rainy afternoon
that you will push through level four
to find the manic spiders and the concert grands
with incisors where the white notes were
have given on a smudgy town,
smoke or low cloud obscuring your score;
where the scuttling aliens went,
the filing masses and their grave roar.
The edges of the screen grow vague;
your finger hesitates on *fire*.

It will be 4pm some January Saturday,
the crowd stood macked and capped beneath
drizzle freezing down the touchline shadows,
we will access the Third Division North,
en route, in theory, for the Stadium of Light
as long as the ball is dancing goalwards
at the gold-thighed captain's feet
– Roy, presumably, or his seven-figure son
dribbling for the dark beneath the terrace roof,
the incidental net preparing to bulge
and GOAL! appear and disappear in gold
across the instant replay. Your fingers
chafe and numb; you can feel the graphic weather
in a front from Accrington to
the heaven of slick-haired wingers,
the caser's lacing printed into your brow.

It will be dark by the time we exit
whatever programme left us here,
beaten on away goals in Reykjavik
or Sofia. The blue fuzz on the idle screen
will light us from our flickering bedrooms
where later we will turn in pyrexial sleep
dreaming ourselves through the alleys and arcades
of a virtual Madrid, lost at five to three,
picked at last to face Real.

CEES NOOTEBOOM
GOLDEN FICTION

Look! The fires are opening.
The heathens fight over a handful of ashes.
Tomorrow I will set out again with my ship.

They are buried, my friends.
Under the trees their bodies continue.
Their souls are many leaves
and they blow.

I hang my face in the wind
and wonder. Why am I so sad
if I expect no more than looking at fires
and the departure of a ship?

The deceiver sits in his room and writes it down.
From which lives does he write? From which time?
Will real life ever come to him,
take him along?

No, it will never take him along.
The deceiver sits in his room and writes
what the voices tell him.

TRANSLATED BY MARGITT LEHBERT & MAARTEN ELZINGA

RUTH SHARMAN
THE DRESS

I wandered through a mansion in my dream
where countless dresses hung from countless rails.
Some were made of velvet, some of silk,
chenille or lace, and some were filmy veils
that slipped beneath my fingertips, soft
and shimmering in shades of white and cream.

I chose one and my husband helped me in.
In cut and shape it differed from the rest,
tapering to a mermaid's tail, its neck
revealing curves I lacked in life.
                              The dress
he hooked me into was my wedding dress,
and it was black and fitted like a skin.

CONNIE BENSLEY
GETTING OUT OF HAND

Experimenting with virtual reality
she calls up a good-sized house, and in it she pops
Rupert Brooke, who comes out of his study
muttering octosyllabics and twisting
his inky fingers through his famous hair.

Remembering his penchant for anguished passion
she summons Charlotte Brontë – but something goes wrong
and it is Branwell who turns up, though it doesn't seem
to matter, and he falls into conversation with Rupert
about the rail service to Lulworth Cove.

They settle down for tea, and here comes Jane Austen
handing round the bread and butter. Cup in hand,
she leafs through a volume of diaries
found on the coffee table. Her eyes widen
and she drops the book with a nervous glance

over her shoulder, but there is no sign
of the author, for Joe Orton (if he is on
the premises) is engaged elsewhere. More figures
materialise, and surely someone will have to wash
the cups – though that doesn't look like a butler

limping in through the French windows, saturnine
and patrician, with a dangerous-looking hound in tow.
Someone who understands these animals is needed a.s.a.p.
and Conan Doyle springs to mind – being also qualified
to advise about the foot – but no, surely that's GBS

cycling bossily up through the garden
ready to sort everyone out, if he can make himself heard
above the shouting and barking. Now they're all
comparing something, and fragments of speech surface:
Missolonghi . . . mosquito . . . my best apple tree . . .

KATHY MILES
NOAH'S ARK

We all make arks against a flood;
the rising tide that slips across the border.
Riding the sea, I think of you,
while the dory slaps against the trough
and we cross the line away from shallow water.
I take that race between my thighs,
as a horse that canters ocean.
I am the figurehead on the prow,
carried on an ark of my own making.

Your face recedes against this world,
and the boat is like a roller-coaster
as we call up gods of sun, rain, weather.
Floating above the mountains of sea,
I am assured the dory is secure,
that our tiny ship will not go down.
A dolphin noses the starboard side.
In the water, slippery and dark,
his head is sleek as a drowned girl.

Two by two they paired the animals,
male and female, dark inside the hold.
Claws are at my jugular; gold lions,
sinuous tigers. Their fear is held
within this house of motion
as they slam the bars, the lack of air
and sunshine. Hard to imprison
so much energy. Beneath the water-line
their passion shakes the current.

Together, we were once a harbour.
Fortressed against the winter cold,
we huddled, sheltered in each other's arms.
Still on bad days I remember
that woman-bride of twenty years,
the warmth of you against my icy palms.
Now there is only silence after storm,
the quietness of an immaculate room;
animals running free when the flood-gates open.

JAMIE McKENDRICK
THE BEST OF THINGS

The lawn wears
a peaked hat
– that'll be

the velvet fellow
brisking with his claws
through the dark shaft

one worm dipped
in strychnine
the farmer said

would do for him
and his whole tribe:
he eats the worm

drops dead
underground then
his sister eats him

dies and so on
till the last one chews
through the last but one

maybe out of respect
like those people
in New Guinea

dying from kuru
after eating
other people

(nature knows best)
or maybe it's just
waste not want not

that'll be it
– digging away there –
have a nice day

JANA STROBLOVA
EURYDICE

From the faint flickering flames of memories
beyond the river of oblivion
(from the soul's underworld)
led out into the light. By day.
He (oh, that roguish smile!)
would even
rob Charon of his coin. Now he made you
walk
blindfold (What is? And what is not?)
with him, behind him . . .

Pity – he no longer looks back!

But you are in the light,
once more in this life!

TRANSLATED FROM THE CZECH
BY EWALD OSERS

ROGER McGOUGH
POET-SPOTTING

On the train to Bangor from Crewe
Jo Shapcott and I, as tutors tend to do
gossip, and get to wonder

which of the passengers are headed
for Tŷ Newydd. That red-headed
punk in tight leather? Unlikely.

More likely the old lady wearing purple
(see Jenny Joseph), daring people
to come close, if any do, they're kissed.

Or, pissed in the corner, surrounded
by throttled cans of Guinness
the man who shakes a mottled fist

at a muse unseen, and screams:
"Orange, orange, there must be
a rhyme for fucking orange!"

P. J. KAVANAGH
AT SWINBROOK

When faith and likelihood collide
you hear no sound, you see a screen
gone suddenly blank, and the computer down.
Years and memories lie coiled inside
unwinking, uninforming green.
He feels himself transparent as these fish
which, heads against the current, wriggle, strain;
his self gone colourless; or his self as seen
by a camera, filmed: a blank-minded man
outside a pub, The Swan, beside the Windrush.

Two talking friends, dear women, briefly gone
to view another church, he's left alone
to work out on his broken-down machine
(he has a fishlike sense of waking-sleep)
what they thought in silence at the stone
named for someone young all three had known,
across the valley. In their ways devout,
all three believers – they believed in what?
That four of them would one day meet again?
Collision. Blankness at the heart of hope,

which contains comfort, strangely. He feels like one
too long a sentry, turned away from the town
peering against the current, while behind
him barracks are dismantled, comrades gone.
As in the biblical room he feels his mind
so swept and cleared new demons might fly in.
The various green, which made him first love England
here, rests on his eyes like a lid and he prays
not to be too-far tested, now he sees,
at least, how beyond-him serious God is.

ELAINE FEINSTEIN
LITTLE VENICE

Sunlight on the canal, seagulls and a few boats
low in the water: this street is no longer
your territory but as I drive through,
the cool remembered glitter conjures you:
that note of surprise in your voice
as you tell of some disaster, your
shoulders shaking in those soft blue
Hemingway roll necks. It was your charm
to have the world become a Truffaut film,
or a Brassens song, in the shared laughter.

"Too clever for your own good", your Cambridge tutor
said, annoyed to have you bypass steady work
in phrasing essays with a casual wit.
I can't remember who it was you hit,
or why the story passed into your legend,
with Paris, Vietnam, and those Insight bylines
which were a part of the same dangerous glamour,
though underneath you were
always lonely in a childhood anger
women never quite escaped.

You startled me on the telephone yesterday
speaking of a dead friend: *"We both loved you.*
You must have known that". What I knew
was the way we lived in one another's
imagination, rather as people in the novels
of Malcolm Lowry. Closer companions
coped with daily behaviour. All the same,
your words reached through an unhappy
morning to restore my stamina.

ADAM THORPE
BIG WHEEL

I feinted with my vertigo and curved
to early middle age, I'd say: anyway
the top. There we stopped and began to sway.
For my idiot daring it was all I deserved.

The remarkable vista of the environs of Gütersloh,
the backs of birds actually in flight, the shrubbery
of trees and the pinhead people made me rubbery
in the legs, of course, but what was worse was the slow

remorseless haul on my brain, or maybe my body
for the earth far below was wide and craving
my entry at whatever price. The kids were waving
and I started to wail, I'm afraid. I clung to the rod

and shut my eyes. You had to hold me tight.
In high air there was no bolt-hole from whatever
sirens were singing me down . . . as if I could sever
myself from this swaying life without a fight.

KATE CLANCHY
RASPBERRIES

The way we can't remember heat, forget
each year the sweat, the hurt, the weightless
shirt on scented skin, and lose
the taste of raspberries, every winter,

but wake and know in sharp July the vein
burning in the curtain, can judge the light,
the block of sun on crumpled sheets
know the blazing world we'll walk in –

was how it was, your touch. Not the rest,
the muddled bed, the drunkenness, just
the first half-stifled, frightened reach,
the sense of something tiny, meshed,

– like that first dazzled flinch from heat
or between the teeth, sharp pips, a metal taste.

THE REVIEW PAGES

Of Bereavement and Affirmation

by Jerzy Jarniewicz

JAN KOCHANOWSKI

**Laments, translated by Seamus Heaney
and Stanislaw Baranczak**

Faber, £6.99,
ISBN 0 571 17597 X

UNTIL RECENTLY WHAT exclusively interested English translators, editors and critics in Polish poetry seemed to be the response of Polish poets to the pressures of post-war history. In consequence, vast regions of Polish literature, particularly older classical works, remained unknown. Now, with the end of this highly politicised situation, there is a chance for those neglected classics to re-emerge in the English language. The recent work of Stanislaw Baranczak and Seamus Heaney makes me hope that this chance will not be missed. Baranczak, an accomplished poet in his own right, is perhaps the leading Polish translator both from and into English. To the long list of poets whose work he has translated (Shakespeare, Donne, Hopkins, Auden, Larkin), Baranczak has recently added Seamus Heaney. It should not come as a surprise then that Baranczak, taking into account also Heaney's longstanding preoccupations with European literature, managed to persuade the Irish poet to cooperate with him on the translations of Kochanowski.

Jan Kochanowski's *Laments*, written for his three-year-old daughter and published in 1580, mark the peak of Polish Renaissance poetry. The English translation closely follows the Polish original, though it seems to respect faithfulness to rhyme and metric patterns more so than to poetic imagery. The translators occasionally leave out, or introduce, certain images, often enriching the poems with concrete and evocative detail as in Lament 7, where the Polish lines "Alas, dowry and its mistress are enclosed in a single chest" (in M. J. Mikos's more literal translation) are rendered by Heaney and Baranczak as:

O sealed oak chest, dark lid, board walls that hide
the dowry and the bride!

The 13-syllable line, the most typical rhythmic format in Polish poetry, in which the majority of *Laments* were written, has been rightly rendered into its English equivalent, iambic pentameter. Full feminine rhymes, another Polish feature of *Laments*, have been mostly translated into what seems the strongest part of the English version, a miscellany of inventive, usually masculine, Heaneyesque rhymes: perfect and partial, consonantal and vocalic. To my ear, however, the English translation tends to depart in some fragments from the elevated diction of the original, which reverberates throughout with Biblical echoes infusing the cycle with characteristic pathos and loftiness (Kochanowski wrote *Laments* a few years after having translated the Psalms). As a result, the English Kochanowski is a poet of much greater clarity and directness than in the 16th century original version, yet his lyricism and intellectual sincerity are equally compelling. It is perhaps worth recalling here that Baranczak in one of his essays gave several, seemingly obvious, but often neglected, commands to translators of poetry: one of which was not to translate poetry into prose, another, not to translate good poetry into bad poetry. *Laments* prove that such a translation, however difficult, is possible. Thanks to the co-operation of the two poets, the reader is offered genuine poetry in English, and, arguably, a very good one.

However, this exquisite cycle of elegiac poems lends itself to the type of dangers that no literary work which takes up the subject of great personal loss can avoid confronting. Literature offers means of articulating personal grief, but at the same time it tends to centre on itself and to develop independently of the initial real-life stimulus, no matter how intense it might have been originally. Inevitably, personal feeling has to struggle with literariness, lyricism with rhetoric. This conflict underlies Kochanowski's *Laments* to such an extent that, as Baranczak notes in his introduction, one critic even ventured the apparently eccentric thesis that Kochanowski's daughter did not exist at all and that the whole cycle was only a "purely technical experiment in funeral poetry". It has to be remembered, however, that Kochanowski lived in an era when imitation was advocated as the desired method of writing. Poets were credited with artistic talent on the basis of their knowledge of Greek and Latin masters, whose work they invoked with quotations, allusions and references. It is thus not by chance that Kochanowski began his cycle with a reference to two Greek thinkers, Simonides and Heraclitus, and ended it with a quotation from Cicero. In *Laments* Cicero plays the role of Kochanowski's alter ego: the Polish poet felt a strong affinity with the Roman orator whose seemingly unshakable stoical beliefs failed to console him after the death of his daughter, Tullia. Other bereaved figures whose bad fortunes provide Kochanowski with analogues for his own predicament include, predictably, Niobe and Orpheus.

References to ancient philosophers and classical allusions, the organisation of the poems into a carefully designed cycle, a whole range of standard rhetorical devices (such as apostrophes, questions, exclamations, series of synonyms and epithets), may leave the reader with a feeling of unease and create the impression of a too finely wrought product of literary craftsmanship. The uniqueness of *Laments* rests, however, on the fact that the poet convincingly managed to yoke convention and formal discipline to passages of great lyrical intensity. It soon becomes clear to the reader that his models were not only the highly conventionalised classical elegies, but also the lyrical "Canzonieri" of Petrarch.

Throughout the poems Kochanowski, interweaving rhetoric and lyricism, conducts the reader through the typical stages of an elegiac journey. The cycle moves from the expressions of the poet's grief after the death of his daughter, through the evocative presentation of everyday scenes from family life when the child was still alive, to the traditional laudatory piece which eulogises the girl's virtues, calling her the "Slavic Sappho". And yet perhaps the most important part of *Laments* is where the poet develops what could be called his intellectual odyssey: here the Renaissance humanist has to confront his now shattered belief in the powers of reason. Becoming aware of the helplessness of all philosophical systems to which he had hitherto assented, the poet begins an angry, bitterly ironic polemic on the main ideas involved in the classical doctrine of stoicism.

While *Laments* does not reveal the poet's early mistrust towards religious dogmas (young Kochanowski came close to Calvinism), these poems do testify to the fact that in the face of a great personal tragedy not only does reason have to surrender, but that often faith also fails. This motif of the religious crisis reaches its culmination in Lament 10 where the mournful father's suppressed doubt is eventually voiced, albeit in the cautious, parenthetical form: "Wherever you may be – if you exist – Take pity on my grief".

And yet this same statement, which might provide evidence of the pain causing the Christian poet to have doubts about the afterlife, again demonstrates the great powers of tradition, convention and rhetoric. For even this outcry of despair turns out, on closer inspection, to be a version of a conventional phrase used in Roman funeral poetry. The poems bring about the overwhelming realisation that everything has already been said; that even when we speak about our most personal matters we are inevitably using other people's words, deeply rooted in the vast plain of tradition. And that these "borrowed words" do not necessarily preclude lyrical intensity, but, on the contrary, often make it possible.

Kochanowski's *Laments* for the death of a child ends with a vision in which not the child but the poet's mother appears before him, to console the poet and teach him how to live with the painful memory of this loss. The authority of ancient philosophers having proved useless, the true knowledge of life is communicated by a woman, the life-giver. The poet, who as a father lamented the death of his child, himself turns into a child, stops speaking and starts listening instead: *Laments* ends with a note of humility, trust and acceptance. However, the instruction from the poet's dead mother does not nullify the doubts and denials which form the substance of most of the preceding laments. The final philosophy of acceptance incorporates the experience recorded in these poems: what should be accepted is not so much the fatality of life, but its human dimension. "Bear humanly the human lot" – and to bear humanly means to experience grief after a loss, not to follow dogmas and not to try to quench the natural feelings of pain and despair. It is precisely at this moment that Kochanowski's critique of stoicism reaches its climax, at this particular moment which also constitutes the culmination of his praise for the joys of family life. The two voices of the lyricist and the rhetorician, the wounded father and the humanist

thinker, sing the two notes of bereavement and affirmation, simultaneously.

Jerzy Jarniewicz is a poet, translator and an editor for *Literatura na Swiecie*.

Beauty and the Beast
by Tim Kendall

DEREK MAHON
The Hudson Letter
Gallery, pbk £6.95, hbk £12.95,
ISBN 1 85235 176 4

READING DEREK MAHON'S first volume *Night-Crossing* alongside Heaney's *Death of a Naturalist*, you might have been forgiven for picking the wrong poet as future Nobel Laureate. Already Mahon was blessed with copious gifts: precocious technical accomplishment, perfect pitch, and a voice which – even if Yeats, MacNeice and Larkin intruded too often – showed signs of maturing into something new and distinctive. By the time his *Poems 1962-1978* appeared, Mahon was established as one of the most important poets in the UK.

Subsequently, something began to go awry. *The Hunt by Night* (1982) and the "interim" pamphlet *Antarctica* (1985) consolidated without really advancing Mahon's reputation. Since then, only his translations of Jaccottet survive comparison with earlier work. Mahon has also channelled his energies into tinkering with old poems (often wrecking them in the process), and producing workmanlike versions of Molière and Euripides. His output suggests a poet keeping his hand in, waiting for the real thing. His admirers have been waiting too; but they will find nothing to satisfy them in *The Hudson Letter*.

There had been warnings of what to expect. 'The Yaddo Letter', now published in this collection, first appeared separately in 1992. Addressed to the poet's children, it contains some embarrassingly bad passages. We discover, for example, that Saratoga Springs has achieved renown because

it was here, in an open field north of the town,
that Philip Schuyler clobbered John Burgoyne
in 1777, two hundred and thirteen years ago,
thus helping to precipitate the America we know.

It gets worse when Mahon hands down wisdom to his offspring, who learn that "life consists in the receipt of life", and that they must respect values "pertaining to the true, the beautiful and the good". When he apologises for sounding "tedious and trite", he needn't expect a demurral.

'The Yaddo Letter' is the longest poem in part one of the volume, which is also made up of translations, the Yeatsian 'Noon at St. Michael's', and a few pieces of light verse. 'River Rhymes' and 'Anglo-Irish Clerihews' have exclusively literary subjects, and thin jokes. Only his Miss Prism clerihew succeeds, easily outshining the others:

Laetitia Prism,
A precursor of "transformative" feminism
Anticipated contemporary refigurations of sexuality
In, and I quote Lady Bracknell, "a three-volume
novel of more than usually revolting sentimentality".

The most important work in *The Hudson Letter* is undoubtedly the title poem, which constitutes part two of the volume. It consists of eighteen sections, mainly voiced for the poet himself, but including monologues by Sappho and Bridget Moore. Occasionally Mahon's internal editor switches off: at one point he announces, with memorable awfulness, that 'I shall walk the Dublin lanes as the days grow shorter, / I who once had a poem in *The New Yorker*'. But a section like 'Beauty and the Beast' (a witty paean to *King Kong*, and Fay Wray in particular), although still falling short of earlier work, at least does enough to remind the reader of former glories. Mahon's achievement is considerable and secure; hopefully, future volumes will be more successful than *The Hudson Letter* in adding to it.

Tim Kendall's study of the poetry of Paul Muldoon will be published by Seren this summer.

Renovated Properties

by Roger Garfitt

JON STALLWORTHY

The Guest from the Future

Carcanet, £7.95,
ISBN 1 85754 132 4

IT IS A BRAVE MAN who uses some of the world's most famous poems as springboards and then proceeds to execute backflips and double somersaults in the original stanza forms. And yet that is what Jon Stallworthy has done, breathing new life into the forms of Browning's 'Childe Roland To The Dark Tower Came', with its two repeated rhymes tolling across six lines, and Pushkin's 'Eugene Onegin', an intricate fourteen-line stanza that rhymes more intensively than a sonnet. Still more remarkable is the way he takes the tongue-tripping cadences of 'The Lady of Shallot' and makes them work in a contemporary context. For these are much more than technical exercises: they are snatches of radio traffic from this century's storms, true stories culled from the lives of friends and shaped into modern folktales.

Tennyson's 'Four gray walls, and four gray towers', become the walls of a hospital where

> the stretchers come and go
> and walking wounded at all hours
> file across the blackened snow

– a brilliant example of how to renovate a Romantic property. 'The Girl from Zlot' is set after the German invasion of Poland and some of the storytelling is inspired, particularly the moment when she and her fiancé

> see a tank
> break cover, growling. Squat,
> reptilian, a second, third,
> fourth, fifth, sixth, seventh snouting head
> sniffs the wind . . .

'The Nutcracker', which tells of the star-crossed love of an English diplomat and a Russian ballerina at the outbreak of the War, makes good use of the filmic freedom that gives narrative verse such an edge over narrative prose, the rapid pace and the lingering focus, the sudden, summary power of an image to transform a scene and fix it at its height:

> She danced a pas de deux with her shadow,
> embroidering the smokey air
> as if the law of gravity had no
> imperial jurisdiction there,
> but other winged heels crossed the meadow.

The title poem is a reflection on the story of Isaiah Berlin's ill-fated visit to Akhmatova in Leningrad in 1945. Stallworthy's achievement here is to create a convincing rhythm for Akhmatova's voice, articulated by mid-line pauses that give it a Sibylline power. His translation of the section of her 'Poem without a Hero' in which Berlin appears as 'The Guest from the Future' is a considerable advance on D. M. Thomas's version in the Penguin *Selected*.

The three wartime poems are drawn together by a fine translation of Nikos Kavadias' 'Marabou', a poem I am glad to discover, based on an unrhymed version by Gail Holst Warhaft. Kavadias was a radio officer in the merchant marine and it is this that gives Stallworthy his central image. He uses it to haunting effect as he brings together the two lives, the translator's and the poet's:

> Marrying her voice to his
> in Ithaca (New York), she learns despair
> deferred, while keeping watch or studying
> the instruments at midnight from his chair.
>
> His odyssey prepares her for her own:
> the bright stars blown out one by one,
> the straits, the rip-tide, watches, instruments
> that monitor the sinking of her son.
>
> The dark is full of voices. Ship to ship
> and ship to shore, they throw a line
> across the waves . . .

Stallworthy could have closed the book there, a heartbreaking ending to a well-integrated sequence. He chooses to continue, via the Minotaur section of Francoise Gilot's *Life with Picasso*, to a portrait of Gilot as 'My Last Mistress' (based on Browning's 'My Last Duchess') and of the artist/poet as a Minotaur retracing the thread to the heart of his own labyrinth.

The Gilot poems seem slight but 'The Thread' is as good an evocation of poethood as I know and makes an adroit use of the 'Childe Roland' stanza:

> a sort of seething in my chest and head,
> as if a swarm of bees had nested
> in a hollow trunk, and were again
>
> about to swarm. I had no memory,
> no notion of how far my feet had still
> to go, no will apart from the swarm's will.

It is an intriguing coda to a collection that shows the resources still latent in traditional forms and reminds us what a versatile instrument narrative verse can be. It should win Jon Stallworthy a new audience for his poetry, after the years of prominence as editor and biographer.

Roger Garfitt's new book is *Border Songs* (Five Seasons Press).

Generous Balloons

by Sophie Hannah

JENNY JOSEPH
Ghosts and Other Company
Bloodaxe, £6.95,
ISBN 1 85224 295 7

THE GHOSTS IN Jenny Joseph's new book are not all ghosts of the standard deceased variety. There are also ghosts from the past, still alive but no longer part of the writer's life:

> . . . you wraiths, who,
> Gone from my life, are having proper
> dinner
> In the flesh, of flesh, elsewhere; and
> towhom
> I may not even be a memory.
> ('Come and Have Dinner')

Jenny Joseph doesn't just pay lip service to the theme of ghosts, she explores it thoroughly, bringing us ghosts from the future as well as the past. In one of the most impressive poems in this collection, 'Ballad of Rodborough Common', a woman sees an apparition of a sinister couple and overhears their disturbing conversation, by the end of which the man has psychologically and emotionally destroyed the woman:

Stuart Redler

> He played. He won. Got up to go
> Leaving her slumped in the chair as dead;

Later in the poem the woman sees the face of the man from her apparition in her lover's face, and runs away. The ghostly couple in this poem have something in common with Dickens' Ghost of Christmas Future in that their purpose is to deliver a warning by showing the woman what she and her lover might become.

Not all Joseph's ghosts are so easily recognisable. In 'The Uninvited', they tell her: ". . . how badly I have done things", and ". . . stand at every corner with lists of things to blame me with".

These "uninvited guests" are not necessarily human. They could be psychological obstacles and insecurities, or is the author paralysing herself by imagining the disapproval of specific people? By the end of the poem: "That terrible gang have gone", but an unsettling feeling remains because we were never quite sure who or what they were.

Joseph shows us that ghosts are as individual as humans. They don't all like to hang out in damp, cobweb-strewn attics. In the poem 'In Honour of Love', she addresses a ghost who, while alive, liked clean, cheerful places, saying to him now that he's dead:

> . . . you would never bear
> Burdens you would not shoulder while alive.
> You'll still want . . . comfort.

This book is about loss and sadness, but it is equally about life and hope. In 'Patriotic Poem Against Nationalism', Joseph addresses a baby:

It is for such as you who everywhere
Turn to their mother's milk, try out the air,
Move away from the glare, that if we could
We would change nations into geography.

This is Joseph at her best, with her syntax sharp
and focused, as in the powerfully abrupt final stanza
of 'Marching Song':

I suppose I could take you along now
Fill in a claim to a past,
You that I fashion into
New friend from old ghost.

In other poems the form is less effective:

          . . . the trees
Are sometimes very beautiful, it's just
It's sad that summer has left us. It's more difficult
To get done the things expected of us. That apart
  It suits me in a way . . .

                              ('A Letter')

Phrases like "the chrysalis of doubt", "balloons
of generosity" and "the remorselessness of Spring"
jarred slightly, but this is a generous-spirited book
and, despite any flaws it may have, my balloon of
generosity towards it remains undeflated.

Sophie Hannah's first collection, *The Hero and the Girl Next
Door*, was published by Carcanet in 1995.

JENNY JOSEPH

ELEMENTAL — NOT TO MIX, BUT HOW THEN?

The principles of anger and of blenching
Are best not switched. How sick, as shrinking violet
Tiger grin is. And obdurately wasted
The sallowed forest windflower's silk skin lifted
On crag to face the noon.

The principles of rashness and of paleness
Are best not mixed. How useless in the foray
The sickened stomach of a decent fear.
Ruinous is the jewelled web as stanchion
Where a crude timber would support a door.

The balance of a milligram brass measure
Is nothing but curio in a sand-bagged city
And worse than curious, to weigh air in the desert.

We are brought up to bend, mix, modify.
We have to, to be human. We are not tigers
And even children with skins as soft as petals
Do not prosper when led to live like flowers.

So we fall twice, hubristic for purity
Rigid for the splendid idea.

To know and move on this
Is counsel of despair – and of survival.

Distressed Perspectives

by Adam Thorpe

DAVID JONES

The Sleeping Lord & other fragments

Faber, £9.99,
ISBN 0 571 17449 3

A Fusilier at the Front

ed. Anthony Hyne,
Seren, £14.95,
ISBN 1 85411 135 3

JONATHAN MILES & DEREK SHIEL

David Jones: the Maker Unmade

Seren, £29.95,
ISBN 1 85411 134 5

I FIRST READ *The Anathemata* from end to end (footnotes and all) while conducting a traffic census to see whether Newbury needed a bypass, some fifteen years ago. Deep in the thickets of classical, historical, mythological, archaeological and geological allusions that make up the poem, yet somehow swept on and through by the extraordinary lyrical power and obsessive sense of urgency the poem has, I no doubt missed a few cars on those little lanes, but the Roman rectilinearity that Jones was so fascinated and repelled by is now, as I write, carving through the various potencies of wood and riverscape that also haunt all Jones's work, both textual and pictorial, and making the great lines from 'A, a, a, Domine Deus' singularly relevant:

I have run a hand over the trivial intersections.
I have journeyed among the dead forms
causation projects from pillar to pylon.

This first poem from *The Sleeping Lord & other fragments*, paperbacked for Jones's centenary year (1995), is not so much a cry as an anguished shrug, failing to find God "at the turn of a civilisation" the poet-painter had already long turned his back upon. Born into a suburban, lower-middle-class family in Brockley, south London, with an artistic if possessive mother and a "very religious" Welsh father (who was, fortuitously, a professional printer), his early gift for drawing was encouraged in a way that now seems remarkable: at fourteen he was already a student at Camberwell School of Art, supported by his parents. One mourns its curriculum, infiltrated by Impressionism and Post-Impressionism while retaining an academically classical base – and it certainly served Jones well. By the time the Great War drew the slight, child-like nineteen-year-old into its ghastly maw, spitting him out four years later with a set of neuroses that, periodically treated but mostly suppressed, would stay with him all his life, his proficiency was impressive. His nephew's collation of his war sketches in *A Fusilier at the Front* is testimony both to that and to Jones's quiet sensitivity of response (the sleeping sergeant, the dead rats, the warming brazier), which tells us more, visually, about the pitiful side of the trenches than the dramatising stuff of an official war-artist like Paul Nash.

The rest of Jones's long life was, in some senses, a painful (and celibate) search for redemption in a smashed world. The two greatest poems in English to come out of the war – a war which defines our century – are *The Wasteland* and Jones's *In Parenthesis* (1937). The one contemplates the wreckage from the non-combatant's guilt-ridden view, the other (started ten years later) testifies as an infantryman, "suffering" the Calvary of humanity's sins. It towers above any other prose or verse memorial of that war (indeed, of any war), and yet was written through the very peak of his other parallel career as engraver, painter, illustrator and sculptor. In 1921, eager to dilute his suburban origins, abruptly shifting class, Jones had entered that peculiarly stifling and intense world of English Catholicism, joining Eric Gill's Ruskinian community at Ditchling and then the remoter Capel-y-ffin, reading the Thomist Jacques Maritain and finding his desire for "significant form" realised in the Incarnation and Passion of Christ, by which the artist's own sign-making is "validated". As Miles and Spiel emphasise in their exhaustive study of his visual work, *The Maker Unmade*, Jones is a unique mixture of the Romantic and the mediaeval, combining "a Romantic susceptibility to nature with a mediaeval capacity to see things as religious signs of something else". (He also replaced the Roman guards around the Cross with cockney Tommies.) "Nature" here is, of course, the British landscape, and particularly its prehistoric and Celtic residues: turning one's back on modern civilisation meant either literal exile or an embracing of the "national pastoral" of artists like John Piper or John Minton, searching (as Spenser and Blake once did in verse, as Hill and Hughes do now) for the deeper sonorities of the mythological voice, rejecting the prattle of progress, rescuing Arthur from child's play and Rackham and placing him firmly in the island's hospitable bed of woods and hills and rivers, her numinous lord. (It is significant, perhaps, that Brockley only lost its last fields during Jones's childhood; his oil-painting of 1926, *Suburban Order*, is a deeply depressing if uncharacteristic account of this shifting of the urban limit.)

But Jones is also, like Joyce and Eliot, a supreme modernist. Only in his later, debris-packed and deeply disturbed drawings like *The Paschal Lamb* or *The Four Queens* (works Miles and Shiel dismiss as "doodles") does he allow his antiquarianism and a Gill-like metaphysical intolerance to close the doors, to paper over the cracks, to proffer pseudo-icons for our saving contemplation. *The Maker Unmade* generally treats with tact Jones's private agonies, quoting Wilhelm Reich helpfully on the question of religious obsession and sexual frustration, and pointing out (with an almost prudish delicacy) the fecund proliferation of phalluses in the later work. Even the great watercolours of the 1930s, from *Mehefin* to *Flora in Calix Light* to *Curtained Outlook*, tremble on the edge of dissolution; the vista – often a stormy sea – threatens to overwhelm us as it never does in the equally fenestrating Bonnard; jugs and flowers, chalices and thorns, candelabras and curtains writhe together on a flattened picture-plane that destabilises our viewpoint, and makes us take the Christian iconography as both celebratory and deeply vulnerable. Yet watercolour is also a soft, translucent medium, full of air and light, offering mystical otherworlds through the fraught pencil-marks and distressed perspectives. The effect is unique, and it is also the effect of his poems: a linguistic, burdened busyness on the page is shot through by a wondrous lightness, a kind of aural serenity laid on like levels of perfectly-applied wash – even when the speaker is a visiting Roman tribune, symbol of the hard and spiritless contemporary world that Jones sets against the supple and creative Celtic periphery:

No dying Gaul
            figures in the rucked circus sand
his far green valley
            more clear than do I figure

from this guard-house door
            a little porch below Albanus.

Miles and Shiel make clear that, as Jones's literary genius grew more interesting to him, so his pictures suffered, becoming less concerned with recreating (transubstantiating) the thinginess of things, and more with the narrative potential of an image. As he wrote to Richard Shirley-Smith, a Jones devotee who taught art at my school (the rooms facing, appropriately, the ancient green flank of "Merlin's Mound", where the mage was supposed to be buried): "I sometimes think that I stopped being a good artist in the 1930s, and since then it's been a kind of aftermath". Some aftermath! Not only the tumultuous epic of *The Anathemata* (trembling with its duality of meaning – "devoted" and "accursed"), but essays, radio talks, these marvellous "fragments" and, of course, the painted inscriptions of the 1950s and '60s, in which he achieved a late resolution of the literary and the pictorial. These unique modernist versions of the "cult-stone", juxtaposing Celtic, Roman, and Anglo-Saxon calligraphy on Chinese white or an abraded mantle of wax crayon, are cleansed of the painterly struggle, the endless corrections, in reproduction, but are still heroic masterpieces of salvage from the heap of "dead symbols" that surround us.

In the same way, 'The Fatigue' in the Faber collection gives new vitality to the Passion by giving us the Tommified voices of the imperial guard on duty that night: like Breughel (or like Auden on Breughel), Jones seeks his truths in the peripheral and the parenthetical, on the spear-carrying, rifle-shouldering boundary between blame and innocence, the weak and the strong, the fallen and the saved. Four years in a world where *limes* [limit, esp. of Roman Empire] and boundaries were matters of life and death, where a welter of sameness, of filth and mud and wreckage, was yet defined down to a quarter of an inch above the parapet, where powerlessness and chance danced nastily together, must have psychologically prefigured his obsession with overlapping *Lebensraum*, with (as he puts it in his essay on the Arthurian myth, speaking of the Celtic Welsh) extending "frontiers the other side of time", or taking legibility and comprehension to its furthest marge.

The Maker Unmade, while afflicted with a ponderous, dry, and often self-conflicting style, eccentric layout and untitled illustrations (as well as getting Jones's birth-date wrong on the very first page), is nevertheless a useful contribution to Jones scholarship, for he has now to be rescued from the coddling arms of his devotees (of which I am one) who tend to the neo-Romantic gush he so skilfully avoided himself. In looking forward to Thomas Dilworth's forthcoming biography from Cape, we must hope that it reveals Jones as the agonised and deeply complex man that he was – a man at the suffering heart of this century, and not just a cult-stone for the few.

Adam Thorpe's latest novel is *Still* (Secker & Warburg). His third poetry collection, *From the Neanderthal*, is forthcoming from Cape.

Out for the Elements

by George Szirtes

JOHN BURNSIDE

Swimming in the Flood

Cape Poetry, £7.00,
ISBN 0 224 04198 3

LAWRENCE SAIL

Building into Air

Bloodaxe Books, £6.95,
ISBN 1 85224 335 X

WALTER PIDGEON, FRANCHOT TONE, Patsy Cline; Katrina, Cathy, Sandra Gillespie. Interfused with eggs, dust, skeletons and scrub, the lost names are drowned in rivers and weirs. There are murders, rapes, doppelgangers and burials (any number of those). Sensuality, guilt and magic tie them all together. This rich dark soil, soaked through with notions of death and resurrection, nurtures a kind of psycho-theology at whose outlines any reader is bound to arrive by a kind of instinct.

John Burnside's imagination contains elements of early Hughes and Redgrove while his diction approaches the almost baroque sensuality of the Heaney of *Field Work*. It relies on metamorphoses, hints of witchcraft, on notions and dreams of gender and family, and exile from these. Above all its antennae are tuned to the buzz and flap of nature, which is beautiful and sinister, but beyond the ordinariness of naming which tries to locate it and keep it in touch with human lives.

In the second part of 'Lack of Evidence', a poem about the murder of a twelve year old girl (the Katrina mentioned above), the murderer speaks:

We are pure souls, buried in flesh,
traces of ether, hanging in a web
of blood and hair,
immersed in muscle, pinned to gravity.
Our life is penance. Death is our release.

The image of the web encumbered soul recurs throughout *Swimming in the Flood*. So do violations: a clear notion of evil in 'Wrong' where the child wishes the father dead but kills small creatures instead with a conscious cruelty, engages with a

questioning face
a stitchwork of horsehair and mortar to hold it together.

The theology posits a lycanthropic male roaming disenfranchised through the world and seeking the witch-female composed of eggs, amulets, "bonnets and nylons, ribbons of freshwater pearls . . . hairpins and beads" who defines the landscape and the language and finds her nearest familiar in the bird of the liberated soul.

With so much witchiness and implied blood one almost forgets the ordinariness from which these people spring. People in Burnside are often presented as shreds of nature, psyches saddled with memories of distant half-understood images. They are not strictly histories but exist in the dimension of their apotheoses as emblems. The world they inhabit is one of sadness and frosting. In that world I am sometimes grateful to see theology give way to the pathos of the infertile woman in 'Barren', of the "darkened rooms, the cups and wireless sets" of 'A Private Life', of the patients in 'In the Psychiatric Hospital', of Franchot Tone, Patsy Cline and of the parents of the murdered girl in 'Lack of Evidence'; in other words of the less conscious actors in the psychic dramas.

However that may be there is no denying that John Burnside writes beautifully. Sean O'Brien characterised Burnside's early poems as "walking the line between scruple and hyperaesthetic affectation". Given his copiousness these dangers are real enough, but less so as the poems move from mythology towards history. Reading the darker poems here – and none of them is exactly light – is like reading Macbeth under water.

Lawrence Sail

The cover of Lawrence Sail's latest book, like his last, the *New and Selected Poems*, is black and uses a Paul Klee painting for motif. This argues a continuity of perception, and the patient, wholly unshowy art of piecing together small fragments in order to make a world does in fact continue to characterise his work.

Building into Air is divided into three distinct parts. The first concerns itself with unnamed cities: three poems bring together snapshots and voices associated with specific places, and these are bedded in among other poems dealing with associated images. Auden is quoted as one of the epigraphs to the section, and it is clear that the poems are as much about citizens and notions of order as about the physical look of cities. The diction, as always, is light and precise and attempts to hold together the sense of disintegration which runs through the poems. The disintegration is partly linguistic. 'The Expedition' forewarns us:

Almost the last
Words of our leader
Had to be heard
In the absurd context
Of whooping birds,
The gibber of monkeys . . .
. . . *We have no authority*,
He said – and the language
Simply came apart.

The polyphony that follows enacts the breaking up without becoming the dominant mode. The quiet, patient voice itself refuses to fragment even as it outlines the conditions for a new Second Coming with Hiroshima as its herald. The elements of post-modern technique do not celebrate Bakhtin's notions of carnival but lament the lack of coherence.

While the cities are full of detail but remain generalised in outline (Klee's vision of bright coloured bricks and tiles are appropriate) the love poems of the second section are clearly specific both in occasion and person, and this gives Sail's lyricism more scope. Key lines from various poems, such as, "Now and then your long / Slender legs show up / In the pale flashlight", "a fighter plane just splinters / The afternoon sky" or "The suitcase gaping under hard

lights" show feeling disposed about moments of vulnerabilty. The word love, when it occurs, is a re-assuring sound, a mantra of sorts to repeat in the face of nervous wonder. The loveliest image here (from 'Seeing Through Water') is, however, one of healing:

It is something about the paleness of your brow,
Your head held just clear of the pool
And turned slightly to one side;
Your arms that meet
And spread, pulling the water back,
And close to meet again.

The best of the love poems are, to my mind, the best of the book. The third section contains poems on various themes and occasions and of various scope. Two of them, 'The Sea Again' and 'The Landscape of Threat', come directly from centre field, the others are a touch insubstantial by comparison. Sail's centre field is an intimate, intelligent and wholly human place and all the more so when he is slightly terrified of losing that which he holds most dear. Despite a climate of linguistic shifts and ironies people continue to feel simply, directly and, sometimes, devastatingly.

Borrowed Plumage

by Helen Dunmore

ALICE KAVOUNAS

The Invited

Sinclair-Stevenson, £7.99,
ISBN 1 85619 781 6

ALICE KAVOUNAS IS the daughter of Greek parents who emigrated to New York, where she was born. In her turn Kavounas left her place of birth, and she now lives in Cornwall. The poems of her intensely personal first collection embody the social, linguistic and geographical dislocations which have shaped her life. One of the most interesting tensions in the book is that between her father's experience and her own. The father, "Americanised, camouflaged in the dull plumage of drip dries", doesn't forget where he comes from, and in time he throws off his borrowed plumage:

> None of us could reach you in those last years.
> You'd escaped from an adopted country to your
> Aivali,
> those childhood orchards, the one sustaining memory.
> ('Abandoned Gardens')

The adjective "sustaining" is particularly suggestive. In this collection, Kavounas seems to argue that true memory sustains, but nostalgia destroys. The point has reverberations well beyond the personal, as the current controversy over language within the USA confirms. Those who lose their language in the process of becoming American may be compelled to fall back on a debilitating nostalgia for a lost culture, a home which is not longer home. Kavounas' father is a man whose name and age have been altered by outsiders. As a child he brought melons to his Turkish teacher, who dubbed him *Kavun*, the Turkish for melon. As an adult, emigrating to New York, he gained a new date of birth:

> 'Date of birth'. Misrecorded indelibly in ink.
> Some lazy, low-level American immigration officer!
> We joined in that conspiracy, celebrating
> shamelessly his slip of the pen, clapping each year

> as you blew out more candles . . . Your alien's fear
> of detection was unreasonable then. I understand it
> now.
> ('Abandoned Gardens')

What Kavounas understands about herself slowly clarifies from poem to poem. Her use of language is precise, even steely, and there is very little self-pity here. 'Chrysler Building' is a fine evocation of a city where the rituals of dereliction are as demanding as those of prosperity:

> The Skateboard Man, his schedule tighter than a
> train's,
> pushes his torso, monkeylike,
> cruising the rush-hour platform, arm jabbing out,
> thigh-high to the crowd.

> The Lint Lady picks, picks, picks, picks, picks . . .
> Naked beneath that torn and matted fur
> her skin flakes, grey ash mixing in the cindery wind . . .

The last poem in the book, 'Home Ground', makes the most of its position. Here, Kavounas confronts head-on the idea of homesickness for a home that does not exist. She casts a light back on a childhood which was in itself an exile because of the child's longing

> . . . to feel like this,
> slowly taking root, inconspicuous as moss,
> right as rain . . .

> Had I known, all those years ago, (but how could I?)
> that one day I'd be here, those journeys would've
> been
> more than counting miles . . . Precisely not to know
> is to be a child . . .

The helplessness of the child, going where it does not want to go, taken away when it would rather stay, is finely balanced against the helplessness that so often lies within the adult's "choice" of emigration.

This collection of poems almost became homeless itself, after being accepted for publication. Kavounas fought the publisher's attempt to break a signed contract, and succeeded in getting *The Invited* published.

Helen Dunmore's new novel, *Talking to the Dead*, is published by Viking in July.

Flying Crooked

by Neil Powell

RODNEY PYBUS

Flying Blues

Carcanet, £9.95,
ISBN 1 85754 073 5

DUNCAN FORBES

Taking Liberties

Enitharmon, £5.95,
ISBN 1 870612 27 2

IAN CAWS

Chamomile

Headland, £6.95,
ISBN 0 903074 59 1

MIKE JENKINS

This House, My Ghetto

Seren, £5.95,
ISBN 1 85411 140 X

TONY CURTIS

War Voices

Seren, £5.95,
ISBN 1 85411 141 8

JON GLOVER

To the Niagara Frontier

Carcanet, £8.95,
ISBN 1 85754 055 7

YANN LOVELOCK

Landscape with Voices

University of Salzburg,
ISBN 3 7052 0433 5

HUGH McMILLAN

Horridge

Chapman, £5.95,
ISBN 0 906772 52 4

WHEN THIS PARCEL of books arrived, I was thinking about Robert Graves – reading the new biographies, re-reading the poems. Despite his alarming eccentricities, what a shrewd fellow he was: above all, perhaps, in his cheerful ability to take on all manner of literary hack-work without allowing it to taint the quite different business of poetry. Not all these eight writers would recognise that distinction as essential or even comprehensible; but then not all of them have the first clue about writing a poem.

Rodney Pybus

It was Graves, of course, who compared himself to "The butterfly, a cabbage-white, / (His honest idiocy of flight)" which, unable to fly straight, has as more than ample compensation "A just sense of how not to fly". The first part of Rodney Pybus's latest collection is populated by butterflies of altogether more aristocratic lineage: they have Latin names or, failing that, evocative English ones – 'Scarlet Admirable', 'Grand Surprize', 'Clouded Yellow', 'Green Hairstreaks'. In fact, these poems are informed by a fusion of two complementary interests: the lepidopterist meets the lexicographer, field-glasses alternate with reading-glasses. Just occasionally, this results in a forbidding density of arcane information: you relish with Pybus a whole flight of delicious butterfly-words, then suddenly realise you don't quite know what the creatures look like after all.

But expertise and literary skill are beautifully balanced, and nowhere more so than in the wonderfully evocative 'Pieces of Fire and Heaven'. This is a poem which focuses and refocuses from its vantage-point among North Norfolk dunes: terns with "white plummeting ripostes"; sea-holly's "bloomed and scratchy leaves"; "overcasting clouds, flung from The Wash" which "scumble dimming blues with greenish greys". At last Pybus seems to glimpse a rare butterfly, only to realise the truth which meshes disappointment with celebration:

> It was only *Icarus* he'd come upon, wings unmelted,
> still on sea-holly leaves, yet, opening, they
> seemed to him at last no small invention, those
>   smalted
> fliers pausing there, common as sky.

Those lines are full of gentle complexities: the understated mythical allusion, the nicely dissonant half-rhymes, the exactness of "smalted", and the subtle paradoxes of "no small invention" and "common as sky".

The second half of the book, 'Words of a Feather', is more remarkable still: here Pybus has taken two treacherous forms – the verse novel and the epistolary novel – and combined them in an 80-page fictional narrative: it looks like pretentious folly and turns out to be a stunning success. It is set in 1935–'6, and its principal characters are Maurice, discovering a new life in Mauritius, and his wife Eleanor, deserted (as she slowly realises) in Suffolk: we get Maurice's letters home and his increasingly besotted poems; Eleanor's affectionate, then despairing letters to her husband; and verse interjections of an unnamed narrator with a voice very like the author's own. Neither Maurice nor Eleanor is entirely attractive. He is eventually reduced to a kind of wheedling disingenuousness to evade the fact that he is living with a now-pregnant lover: he hasn't, he insists, "gone native like some painter in the South Seas", but

> It's to do with Europe and England
> and this tiny fragment of Empire,
> what it might mean to be
> 'civilised' and 'cultured'. We use
> these slippery words much too easily.

Or, at any rate, Maurice does: the poem's approach to such matters is thus ironically mediated through the voice of a thoroughly unreliable narrator. But Pybus also shows Eleanor veering from tweeness (the "terrible hooter" of the liner at the quayside is "the ship clearing / its throat to say Goodbye") to histrionic despair ("Yes, I am getting hysterical, since / you don't ask, and / I drink more than is good for me"). This even-handedness is a crucial factor in making 'Words of a Feather' both engaging and engrossing; like all the best fictions, it is pleasurably re-readable too.

Duncan Forbes

I've admired Duncan Forbes' work ever since I read his poem 'Ex Officio' – a bitter-sweet piece about a newly-appointed Headmaster's inheritance of his predecessor's garden, with its raspberries and their canes – which was among the most accomplished of the excellent Cellar Press series, well over twenty years ago. However, like many of his contemporaries, he's inclined to dress himself in robes borrowed from the late Librarian of Hull, and he knows it:

> 'This was Mr Larkin's style. It stayed
> Consistent all his time with Faber, till
> They lost him.' Disappointments, hopes that fade,
> Pair up with minor failures of the will . . .

There's a lot of old Larkin – undeceived dourness edged with faint sentimentality, predictable metres and rhymes managed with deft self-mockery – in Forbes's latest collection: enough to make one wonder yet again whether this isn't simply the natural voice of English poetry since Larkin, or Auden, or even Wordsworth. When it doesn't quite work, it's because the self-deprecation has been painted on one coat too thickly: for instance, in the poem which begins "Here's a picture of me in a po-faced pose", we ought to have been shown the po-facedness rather than merely being told about it; while the doggerel (or should it be catterel?) of 'Cat Pepper War' is just too silly about its own silliness.

What Forbes does perfectly (and again it's a Larkinesque mode) is the kind of poem which builds up the cumulative detail of a scene, typically through four six- or eight-line stanzas, in order to give it a redefining wrench in the last few lines: 'Ex Officio' was one such poem, and 'The Way Things Are' is another. He's on a cross-channel ferry, apparently describing the outlandish strangers he sees around him:

> Back in the cafeteria-lounge, the youth
> In Megadeth T-shirt and blue neckerchief,
> The skull-and-crossbones buckle on his belt,
> And reading Isaac Asimov is my son.
> The girl with hiccups, sipping Diet Pepsi
> And wearing a pink T-shirt, is my daughter.
> Black cut-off jeans, blue watch-strap, pony-tail,
> She's playing Guns N' Roses on a Walkman.

That combination of alienation and tenderness strikes me as totally authentic and (hence) genuinely touching; his wife, of course, is meanwhile reading E. M. Delafield's *The Way Things Are*. At the end of the poem after the bilingual safety announcements, he imagines "what would happen if", briefly envisaging himself as "hero and apologist / For love so long denied and ill-expressed".

This is "mainstream" poetry in the best sense, making skilful use of established forms to illuminate recognisable aspects of contemporary life; 'Gironde July', neatly counterpointing a 'wide and mud-brown tidal estuary' with a need for 'cold lager and iced lemonade', is another success in much the same manner. *Taking Liberties* is a thoroughly enjoyable collection: intelligent, humane, and well-crafted, even if padded out with a few amiably dampish squibs.

Ian Caws's

shaping spirit is less mid-period Larkin than early Hughes: the poems in *Chamomile* contain resilient codgers, old soldiers, frosty landscapes and even a martyrdom (St Nicholas Owen rather than Bishop Farrar). He's a gentler poet than Hughes, of course, as the first stanza of 'Fishing Off a Wreck' illustrates:

> Through that window, the brown river lunges
> Like an animal. In my glass, stillness,
> Translucence. They are in from the weather,
> These fishermen, crunching jokes in their jaws,
> And in them stirs what makes the sea lather,
> What in my glass makes for more than coolness.

That opening seems seriously underpowered – what sort of brown? which animal? – yet the restrained tone allows "crunching jokes" its surprising force and "what makes the sea lather" its oblique, mysterious effectiveness. Indeed, Caws's most distinctive quirk is his fondness for what might be called the diminutive simile, in which a large object (such as "sea") is juxtaposed or compared with something smaller ("lather"): "curtains . . . Like bar codes", "leaves like corn-flakes", "waves tucking themselves in", "arrows, black hyphens". It's an effective trick, especially when the comparison is compressed into an unexpected verb: "All round, trees fuss in a light wind". Occasionally, one may want to voice mild dissent: "The notes went before him like stepping stones", writes Caws of Vaughan Williams; but they didn't, they came after him. The poem, quite effectively, has the composer walking into immortality on his music; yet it's the art which survives the man, not the other way round.

Mike Jenkins

A curiously brutalist blurb and a quoted review calling Mike Jenkins "one of the wild men of poetry"

prepare the reader for something a good deal more corrosive than *This House, My Ghetto* turns out to be. It's true that there are stabs at social satire, but the real world is probably barmier and nastier than anything in Jenkins's quite kindly imagination. His 'Catalogue for Those Who Think They Own Everything' ("'Don't Let The Bastards Get You Down' ties, / thermal pants with an 'Up Yours!' motif") is absolutely no match for Innovations; while the title-poem, an honourable attempt to get inside the claustrophobic alienation of a British-born "Paki" ("'You don't belong . . . fuck off home!'"), terrorised in what is actually his "home town", betrays its distance in the weak repeated line, "I know how a girl must feel".

Sometimes he seems merely sentimental. In 'New Houses on Georgetown' he attempts a muted polemic about urban redevelopment; terraces with "doors open to wiped feet" have been replaced by new houses "with guarding brick hedges":

> Detached, their only contact
> seems with Outer Space,
> so I wonder if aliens
> have moved in and perhaps
> the red boxes are buttons
> some extra-terrestrial force
> will one day press.

We may charitably assume that he doesn't really wonder anything so daft; nevertheless, he must know that even detached houses actually touch the ground and that open doors might invite unwiped feet. Arguably valid anger is sacrificed to jokey imprecision and, as so often in this book, the language doesn't venture beyond the commonplace.

Tony Curtis

"All wars is sin, sergeant", says rational Attercliffe to John Arden's deranged Musgrave: that might have stood as epigraph to Tony Curtis's *War Music*, an ambitious set of variations on the theme of war – all wars – in the twentieth century. The enterprise is admirable, the execution pedestrian. Many of the poems are just too tightly stuffed with secondary material; others are laboured and over-explicatory. 'Crane-Flies', to take a straightforward example, draws an implicit parallel between insects dismembered by schoolchildren and "mangled corpses parcelled in sheets" in Beirut. I find that comparison unpromising in any case, but it isn't assisted by lines like these:

> This year so many crane-flies
> – Daddy-long-legs –
> each room in our house has a pair.
> They whirr and tick, crucify
> themselves in high corners, against lamps.

The parenthetical gloss seems redundant and in any case could hardly warrant a line of its own, while "crucify" is simply inaccurate (so, indeed, is "against lamps": living crane-flies bump against them, but dead ones end up dangling elsewhere). The trouble is that in his brave attempts to offset the elegiac with the demotic, Curtis continually tumbles towards bathos: for instance, his movingly direct elegy for 'Great Uncle Charlie' is undermined by prosiness:

> The last time we saw him alive,
> a week before Christmas,
> was in the cottage hospital, flanked
> by two of the dying, the obviously dying . . .

Though Curtis's patient observation and essential decency are never in question, they haven't been distilled into memorable poetry.

Jon Glover

Something of the sort might also be said of the prosier parts (some of them actually printed as prose) of Jon Glover's *To the Niagara Frontier,* another extended sequence of variations on a theme: here, though, the starting-point is more promisingly the author's exploration of one part of the USA and its historical, geographical and familial resonances. This has a distinguished antecedent in Donald Davie's *A Sequence for Francis Parkman*; and in poems such as 'Fort George, Fort Niagara, Fort Mississauga' and 'Orders to the Niagara Frontier' Glover comes close to matching Davie's sonorous yet earnestly puzzled tone:

> The orders keep coming to light
> even after so long, this long, when those garrisons
> and camps and histories seemed all lost,
> unpronounceable
> names in the comforting, deathless past. Dead
> metaphors,
> and without compassion? I fear. I fear the frozen,
> travelling words. And I never knew such distances.

Glover is good, too, on the oddly defamiliarising details of the present: buying "maple / candies and cans of syrup from / the farm fridge at Pumpkin Hollow"; being instructed to "Just run your ass backwards in" when parking at a fairground; peering "through the tiny, thick pane" at the back of a TriStar, trying to make sense of the world below.

Yann Lovelock

is a bewilderingly various poet, and this peculiar-looking book (with its disordered prelims, hopeless typography and preface battily labelled "Intro. Essay") isn't designed to assuage bewilderment; nor are such features as a dedication to "Ann, my companion thru so many landscapes" and a poem beginning "swans &. sea. sun." going to reassure those unimpressed by the outmoded illiteracies of what was once called the avant-garde. This is a pity, however, because Lovelock is often a subtle and observant writer with an exact ear for the poetic line:

> Alarm of the hook-billed curlew circling
> marshes after the dry day's horse-fly lance

for instance, or:

> Luminous sunset, in eastward dusk
> a hill's lip is moistened with flame

It's the knack, sustained through so many of these poems, of being simultaneously rapt and sharp-edged which is so impressive. Lovelock writes, "I suppose I'm a Wordsworthian at heart": Coleridgian, I'd have said, which is better still.

Hugh McMillan's

collection opens with a pastiche blurb for 'The World Book of the McMillans'; but almost everyone has heard of these ludicrous books, and plenty of jokes have been made about them already. There's a lot of laddish jokeyness here, some of it quite well aimed, which would doubtless go down well if read aloud; there are also hints, in poems like 'The Fire and the Flowers' and 'Readings of October', of a quieter and (hence) more confident voice. Generally, to return to Graves and his butterfly, the book is stronger on honest idiocy than on flight.

THE SONNET HISTORY

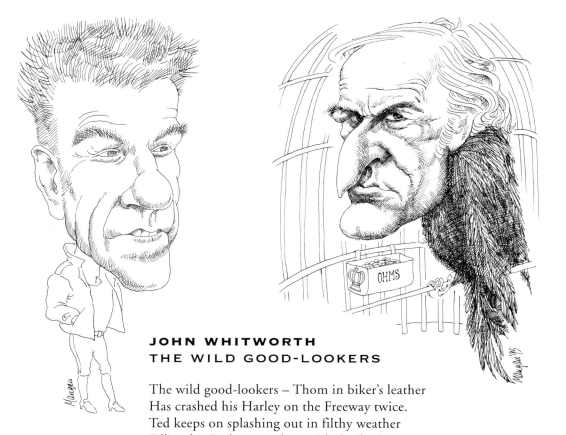

JOHN WHITWORTH
THE WILD GOOD-LOOKERS

The wild good-lookers – Thom in biker's leather
Has crashed his Harley on the Freeway twice.
Ted keeps on splashing out in filthy weather
Filling his Barbour pockets with dead mice.

A poet's life is lived along the edge
Of savage rhythms and primeval surges.
We feel it when our neighbour trims his hedge
And won't sweep up the clippings from the verges.

To hell with smug, suburban platitudes –
We're on the move and Man, we gotta go.
What is it hunches on the gate and broods?
It seemed to be a hawk but it's a crow.

The neolithic forest sleeps beneath.
We were not born to die in Haywards Heath.

New Zealand Cool

by Emma Neale

DINAH HAWKEN

Small Stories of Devotion

Arc Publications, £6.95,
ISBN 0 946407 90 8

A WORK WHICH has been consolidated from the jottings and fragments of an author's journal runs the risk of appearing unstructured, piecemeal, and even beset by trivia. The notebook quality of *Small Stories of Devotion,* however, is part of Dinah Hawken's consecration to the whole process of daily living. As a memorial to a friend, this collection offers a celebration of the everyday, the epiphanic, and the moments of intersection between the two.

The discrete prose poems in this hauntingly illustrated collection become anything other than discontinuous, as images, character descriptions and themes recur in the manner of symphonic motifs – building up structural coherence and towards the exposition of certain spiritual, ethical and philosophical beliefs.

Hawken (whose first collection won the 1987 Commonwealth Poetry Prize for Best First Book), has a diction which is simple and declarative, true to her opening address to the reader ("I'll stop shuffling under my New Zealand cool, I'll come out / and tell the stories in an eager, child-like way"). Yet it deliberately embraces complexities. These can range from cryptogrammatic absences to the avoidance of heavy-handed interpretation of events, to the use of line breaks and games with nuance. Each instance of complexity asks for hesitations and re-runs over single words and syntactical possibilities; an experience that chimes in with Hawken's broader impetus, which is to encourage our perception of other possibilities beneath the plane of ordinary existence.

Hawken's ear is most attuned to the stitching together of sounds in relaxed speech. Her work specialises in the gentle alliteration and assonance embedded in the body of sentences and which thread over line breaks; a fluid music rather than the boxed structures of traditional forms. The intellectual premise which Hawken asks us to accept before encountering this particular music is crucial: "that the unconscious / is fresher and less contaminated by history than history". The following records of "dreams, myths and events", she believes are the closest she can come to any claim to truth. The existence of the unconscious beyond any influence of culture is perhaps a utopian ideal: but such utopian dreams help to inform and impel Hawken's political conscience. Much of what the poems crescendo towards is the possibility of breaking down antagonisms between perceived social opposites.

It is Hawken's particular gift that just as her language attains an intensely symbolic level, she can successfully deflect from the obscure to remind us of our own physical actuality. An early instance of this is her representation of a moment of entry into a new life, evoked by the dream image of mounting a monolithic sphere – "Perhaps it is a breast?" This symbol converts in the next verse, to the clinical reality of a woman's experience of mastectomy – a transition which ultimately deepens the symbolic import, as it reinforces that conventional archetypes have their roots in the most powerful and basic of human experiences.

This bisection of one plane by another can occur in any sequence. Hawken is not only seeking the spiritual in the ordinary – equally she will make a sudden leap from lyrical meditation to the placement of character in a socio-economic reality:

Who is she? . . . She is the context, the swell,
the breathable air. She is singing,
she is swinging the boy on a swing
in the park. She is fluent and steady and unpaid.

The volume moves on to articulate unity in disparity; portraying, with quirky humour, the unlikeliest of couples and larger groups – most of whom, in the absurd way of dreams, lie peacefully together in beds placed against impossible settings. 'Bed' becomes sensual, although not necessarily sexual – an image which gradually unfolds into an achingly fragile symbol of harmony:

Here they are now like a wave in the wide bed:
a woman curving round the spine of a woman
who is curving around the spine of a man
who is curving around the spine of a woman
who is curving around the spine of a child.

Such stark pictorial clarity through language is integral to Hawken's programme for effecting equality. Achieving purity of diction itself embodies the possibility of achieving a new innocence in human relationships. Language may not be where deceptions begin, but it is the medium through which falsehoods are perpetuated. It is the poet's duty, therefore, to use language to create versions of ourselves anew.

Emma Neale has recently started a study of expatriate New Zealand women authors, which will include the poetry of Fleur Adcock.

MONIZA ALVI
NEVER TOO LATE

There are things you don't think about
before you blow up Parliament.
You are so concerned with the barrels of gunpowder
stashed away in the cellar under the coal and wood,
the rickety steps, the crates to shift,
you forget all about the phonecalls to return,
the memos to type, the papers to staple,
the thoughts you were supposed to carry
from one hemisphere to the other.
For years you believed you were an alchemist.
In time you became a firework-maker.
You toyed with firecrackers, rockets, starbursts,
drove the birds right out of the world.
You longed to blow up a sovereign,
a minister, to madden a legislator –
make decent people shout in the street.
Surely you knew you'd be tortured and hanged.
You looked around for someone to blame.
It was Catesby, you whispered. *Robert Catesby.*
You'd had a lifetime of detonation.
They invited you to the firework-makers' last supper.
There was always a sparkle in your stomach,
a star in your brain – the opportunity to give
vivid displays to a captive audience.
But you knew it was never too late.
Never too late to creep down to the cellar
and deal with Parliament.

Outbackstabbing

by Michael Hulse

The Bloodaxe Book of Modern Australian Poetry

ed. John Tranter and Philip Mead,
Bloodaxe Books, £10.95,
ISBN 1 85224 315 5

IN 1992, WHEN I was in Australia to do readings, the War of the Anthologies was raging at full blast. The papers and magazines were full of reviews of two rival anthologies that had recently appeared, *Australian Poetry in the Twentieth Century* (edited by Robert Gray and Geoffrey Lehmann) and the Tranter/Mead *Penguin Book of Modern Australian Poetry*, which Bloodaxe have now put out for the British market under their own name.

Robert Gray is one of the most exciting poets currently writing in English anywhere, with an instinct for rhythm as enviable as Muldoon's, and long overdue for British publication. Lehmann was finally seen here last year when Faber did *Spring Forest*, a revision of his 1978 classic *Ross's Poems*. John Tranter, once the *enfant terrible* of Australian poetry, has been at the forefront of experiment in the registers of poetry, incorporating everything from the idiom of sociology to the random linguistic selection made possible by computer games, and is also overdue for British publication. Philip Mead, a poet too, is Tranter's anchor in Melbourne academia, to offset the Sydney-centrism of the traditional Oz view.

The two anthologies reflect the split in Oz poetry, a split that divides the Murray camp (in which Gray and Lehmann emphatically belong) from the Tranter camp, and Sydney from Melbourne. These divides appear in the two books as opposed ideas of what the Australian poetic tradition means. While both have the same historical catchment (the first landmark poet in each being Kenneth Slessor), Tranter/Mead are hostile to what they perceive as the conservative wing of Oz poetry: they haven't quite the gall to omit Murray, Gray and Lehmann, or others in the conservative line such as James McAuley, Judith Wright and Gwen Harwood, but they drop Douglas Stewart, R. D. FitzGerald and Jamie Grant, all of them anti-Sydney decisions. Stewart, the New Zealand-born

editor of the Angus and Robertson list in the Sixties, had a genial influence on the shape of Australian poetry far beyond Sydney, and was himself a wonderful poet, whose 'B Flat' is among the most amiable triumphs scored by the iambic tetrameter in this century. Gray and Lehmann print it.

Gray and Lehmann have a defence of plural taste that makes perfect sense: "We do not believe literary innovation is necessarily more admirable than an individual, revitalised use of tradition. But neither can we accept the complacencies of much formalism. Beneath both the open and formal approaches, the same qualities of feeling and intellect, and the same visceral abilities, finally justify a poem". Though their 450-odd pages may not contain as many poets as Tranter/Mead's equally ample selection, they seem both more generous and more given to thoughtful re-assessment: where Tranter/Mead, unable to omit A. D. Hope, base their selection on the usual anthology pieces ('Australia', 'Imperial Adam', 'The Death of the Bird'), Gray/Lehmann show a greater scruple in choosing (among others) 'The Double Looking Glass', 'Ode on the Death of Pius the Twelfth' and 'On an Engraving by Casserius', poems which have come to be seen as the heart of Hope's work.

The strength of the Tranter/Mead anthology is implied in Gray/Lehmann's omissions. The first is a curiosity: Tranter/Mead print the complete poetry of "Ern Malley", the hoax poet created by James McAuley and Harold Stewart in the Forties in a fit of aversion to the apocalyptic, automatic styles then fashionable. In my view, their decision to do this is a trendy bit of academy-pandering: well aware that postmodern theory currently favours pastiche as a viable form in its own right, they are hitching a provocative ride on the bandwagon. The "Ern Malley" poems were meant to be factitious, pretentious, and plain daft, and that is still exactly how they read.

But Tranter/Mead's broader policy decision to select generously from Australian postmodern poets – both from the Melbourne writers excluded by Gray/Lehmann (such as Robert Adamson, Gig Ryan and John A. Scott) and from writers elsewhere who are associated with them, such as S. K. Kelen in Canberra or the mercurial John Kinsella in Perth – makes a lot of sense. John Forbes, the Melbourne doyen of Oz postmodernism, gets just two poems in Gray/Lehmann, but Tranter/Mead print nine, and they're right. In one poem, 'Speed, a Pastoral', he looks back to the anti-Keatsian hero of Oz modernity, Michael Dransfield, who died of an overdose in his mid-twenties in 1973 (and is enshrined with twelve poems in Tranter/Mead):

> I think he died too soon,
> as if he thought drugs were an old-fashioned teacher
> & he was the teacher's pet, who just put up his hand
> & said quietly, "Sir, sir"
> & heroin let him leave the room.

Tranter, like Fielding in *Tom Jones* before him, has had tremendous fun at the expense of the extended Homeric/Miltonic simile, and Forbes's lines, in picking this up and also in continuing the idolisation of Dransfield, are a consolidation of Oz postmodernism's own conventions.

The war of the camps could easily be overstated, but it's real and it's continuing, and the shifts in the balance of power depend on the same vexing questions of whose bottom is on which chair, as in Britain. Jamie Grant, for instance, who recently started up the best new poetry list in Australia for Heinemann, recently succeeded Tranter as poetry editor of *The Bulletin*. But none of this politicking need interest a British reader too much – the poetry's the thing. Ideally a reader who wants to know about Australian poetry will buy both the Bloodaxe and the Gray/Lehmann anthology, since they complement each other superbly. (*Australian Poetry in the Twentieth Century* is published by Heinemann Australia in hardback, and as a Minerva paperback, ISBN 1 86330 184 4). Comparing the youngest poets in the two books is a good way of seeing just why it's important to make room for both. Gray/Lehmann end with Jemal Sharah (born 1969). Of Irish and Lebanese extraction, she is Les Murray's god-daughter, wrote a thesis on Spenser, and recently did an impeccable first book with Heinemann, *Path of Ghosts*. Very much in the anti-condescension camp as far as ghetto feminism and ethnic correctness go, she refuses to have anything to do with anthologies that are for women only or kowtow to the new multi-cultural orthodoxies (as seen in the Tranter/Mead book). Tranter/Mead end with the west coast rising star John Kinsella, one of the most exhilarating young poets anywhere at his best, and on his off days utterly incomprehensible. Any reader, in Oz or in Britain, ought to be able to read Sharah's moral and intellectual deliberations, in verse of formal polish, with as much (albeit different) pleasure as the rhapsodic and associative flashes of Kinsella.

Connect, and then Disconnect

by Sujata Bhatt

A. K. RAMANUJAN

The Collected Poems of A. K. Ramanujan

OUP, India, £13.99,
ISBN 0 19 563561 2

SUDESH MISHRA

Preparing Faces
Modernism and Indian Poetry in English

Flinders Press, South Australia,
ISBN 0 7258 0578 1

The Oxford Anthology of
Modern Indian Poetry

ed. Vinay Dharwadkar and A. K. Ramanujan,
OUP, India, £11.99,
ISBN 019 562865 9

ADMIRERS OF A. K. RAMANUJAN'S poetry will be heartened to learn that at his sudden and untimely death he left one hundred and forty-eight unpublished poems (except for eleven which first appeared in magazines) on three computer disks. These new poems, written between 1989–1993, have been read, selected and arranged by eight editors who were all, in different capacities, very close to Ramanujan and to his work. Fortunately, the poems in the computer were already in their final stage, having been initially hand-written and then extensively revised. Sixty of these poems comprise the last section: *Book Four: The Black Hen* of the posthumously published *Collected Poems*. The remaining work, we are promised, will be published separately in a volume of uncollected poems. Readers of *Poetry Review* would know, of course, who Ramanujan was and would also know that his first three collections of verse in English were *The Striders* (1966), *Relations* (1971),and *Second Sight* (1986).

The poems in *The Black Hen* are remarkable in the way that all of Ramanujan's poems are remarkable: there is the same precision, the clarity and

control, the irony, the sharp images, the spare language, and the seamless fusion of paradoxical ideas often arising from various cultural traditions. On the surface these new poems seem to be very simple – re-reading them however, one discovers layers of meanings and a certain energy, a vitality that resonates and makes the poems live differently in the reader's mind each time they are read. There is something chilling in *The Black Hen* poems: there is a preoccupation with death, nothingness, zeros, fear and pain – perhaps influenced by Ramanujan's fascination with Buddhism. The speaker in many of the poems seems to be overcome by sadness and a genuine despair that cannot be soothed by witty or wry overtures. Consider, for example, the following stanza from 'Birthdays':

> Birth takes a long time
> though death can be sudden,
> and multiple, like pregnant deer
> shot down on the run.
> Yet one would like to think,
> one kicks and grabs the air
> in death throes as a baby
> does in its mother's womb
> months before the event.

Although death is thought of in terms of birth and therefore (death) is meant to be seen as something positive, the reader feels uneasy, even frightened by the images.

Two other poems I am intrigued by which also express fear but in a very different way have to do with life and art. The first is the title poem, 'The Black Hen', which I had originally read in *Poetry Review* Vol. 83, No. 1, and which had truly haunted me. The second, more subtle and more mazelike in its movement, is 'Museum':

THE BLACK HEN

> It must come as leaves
> to a tree
> or not at all
>
> yet it comes sometimes
> as the black hen
> with the red round eye
>
> on the embroidery
> stitch by stitch
> dropped and found again

and when it's all there
the black hen stares
with its round red eye

and you're afraid

MUSEUM

As people who appear in dreams
are not themselves, the horses
are not horses in the Chinese painting
that prance out of the walls
to trample the flowers
in the emperor's gardens
night after night.

In her book, *The Cure of Poetry in an Age of Prose,* the American critic and poet Mary Kinzie writes: "It is not simply that poetry eats one away (although this is the case). More to the point might be the reverse: that one weakens and exhausts poetry every time one succeeds in it. The danger in finishing is that one must confront a gap in possibility . . . The better the work – truer to fate and experience – the emptier the maker's life without it. The now complete and self-sufficing poem departs into another sphere. In its place is the lunar landscape of forbidden matter, untouchable, unrepeatable. What has been expressed is now true only for the reader, not for the writer, who cannot keep doing the same turn. And yet the writer's whole working method is based on constancy and repetition . . . the cycles of composition repeat themselves, on the one hand plunging the poet into revulsion at achieved form, and on the other obliging the writer, as if no such revulsion existed, to chafe the cold limbs to life with an energy of undiminished love". Kinzie's description of a writer's dilemma immediately came to my mind when I read *The Black Hen* poems. The black hen lives within the poem through its ability to terrify. But why must the black hen be frightening? And if the horses are not horses, then what are they? Perhaps one aspect of the speaker/dreamer/artist himself. Here, the finished products have acquired an incredible power over the maker. The living poem threatens the very being of the poet. On an another level, it's as if the poet (seeking to go beyond all that he has already written) has probed so far into the unknown depths of his soul that what he encounters is ultimately too powerful to be harnessed into art. The

reader senses the struggle. It is almost as if the poem is stronger than the poet: as if the poem "knows" the poet better than the poet "knows" the poem and as if the poem "knows" the poet even better than the poet "knows" himself. Art is then anything but quiet, unchanging perfection. Even Wallace Stevens' poem, 'Earthy Anecdote' (which I could not help thinking of) is comparatively peaceful, for the clattering bucks seem to disappear into the horizon and the bristling firecat eventually closes his "bright eyes" and goes to sleep, unlike the black hen and the horses in Ramanujan's poems. Has the mask been dropped? Do zeros and nothingness come before or after such turbulence? These are just some of the questions that preoccupied me after reading Ramanujan's newest work.

Sudesh Mishra's doctoral dissertation (written between 1985-1989) takes its title *Preparing Faces* from his chapter devoted to Ramanujan's work. Thus, one may conclude that Ramanujan (accurately presented by Mishra as a master of the persona poem) is a central figure in 'Modernism and Indian Poetry in English'. The other nine poets discussed in Mishra's study are: Nissim Ezekiel, Arun Kolatkar, Keki N. Daruwalla, R. Parthasarathy, Arvind Krishna Mehrotra, Adil Jussawalla, Gieve Patel, Jayanta Mahapatra and Kamala Das. This is a well-written, well-thought-out thesis that manages to avoid jargon. It will certainly be useful for students of Anglo-Indian poetry. One does not need to agree with all of Mishra's interpretations in order to enjoy this book. Those who are interested in a wider range of twentieth century Indian poetry can turn to the ambitious anthology edited by Vinay Dharwadkar and A. K. Ramanujan. (Here it should be mentioned that Dharwadkar, considered to be Ramanujan's most brilliant student, is a superb translator, poet and critic in his own right.) This anthology presents twenty poems originally written in English alongside one hundred and five translations of poems from fourteen languages. The only other anthology of modern Indian poetry that covers all the major languages (via translation) is *In their Own Voice* (focusing exclusively on work by contemporary Indian women poets) edited by Arlene Zide. In the Dharwadkar and Ramanujan anthology each poet is represented by one poem, which obviously makes it difficult for the reader to become acquainted with any one writer's work. But such is the fate of the anthologised! The translations are excellent, as one would expect from Dharwadkar and Ramanujan, who have also collaborated with other gifted translators for the languages they do not know. Nonetheless, while reading this anthology I found myself wishing I knew at least five more languages.

It is indeed tragic that Ramanujan did not live to see this book in print – especially as it was one of his pet projects. Dharwadkar ends the preface with a poignant note and provides a highly informative afterword on modern Indian poetry and its contexts.

The editors (in their humble way) do not claim to have produced "the definitive anthology". Of course their choices are not accidents – still they call it an *open* anthology meant to be taken as a *beginning*: a beginning that should open up space for questions and opportunities for new dialogues and new choices. There will be more anthologies. I believe Vinay Dharwadkar is already working on the next one.

Dynastic Span

by Susheila Nasta

The Heinemann Book of African Women's Poetry

ed. Stella and Frank Chipasula,
Heinemann African Writers Series, £6.99,
ISBN 0 435 90680 1

THE PUBLICATION OF this anthology of African women's poetry marks an important milestone in the history of the publication of African women's writing. Whilst it is perhaps over ambitious in its aim to redress a whole history of exclusionary practices in the representation of women's voices from across the continent, the collection is sensitive in its editorial approach and worthy in its intention to give voice and literal space to several generations of female poets who have remained consistently invisible. As the editors of this anthology, Stella and Frank Chipasula, make absolutely plain, all previous collections of African poetry, including the supposedly pioneering *Penguin Book of Modern African Poetry*, edited by Moore and Beier and now in its third edition, have repeatedly failed to provide adequate representation of women. Paradoxically, whilst woman as "Mother Africa" or Earth Mother, has been an important and recurrent icon or trope in African poetry by men – poets such as Leopold Senghor of the Negritude movement are famous for their nationalistic worship of African woman's black body as the land of Africa for instance – the voices of women themselves have been conspicuously absent both from critical debates and in the selections of editors. This book then, which is "the only anthology of African women poets in existence to date", is crucial in its attempt to retrieve and gather together women's voices from across the

continent, a geographical area which represents a vast poetic landscape. It is also a celebration of the enormity of the racial and cultural diversity of the continent making inclusive areas which are frequently isolated in critical discussions of African writing such as the Islamic Arab North and Egypt.

The range and geographical coverage is impressive. In addition, the editors have provided a number of excellent translations of poetry from previously Francophone or Lusaphone areas. There are also some fascinating short pieces such as the obelisk inscription by Queen Hatshepsut (the earliest poem in the collection), who reigned as a male pharaoh in the Eighteenth Dynasty at the peak of Egypt's power. The voices by women included range then from ancient Egypt to modern Southern Africa, from a celebration of the oral function of women's poetry as sung songs and stories to the political role of some of the previously silenced Lusaphone voices such as that of Aldo do Espirito Santo (interestingly misrepresented as a male voice in the Moore-Beier anthology mentioned earlier).

Such misrepresentations are serious and have unfortunate repercussions. However, as the editors of this anthology make apparent time and time again, it is not just a question of misguided misrepresentations in the odd anthology. The pattern is repeated throughout African literary criticism – in author bibliographies, reference works and critical books. This book deserves praise for its painstaking excavation of a whole wealth of material that has been in danger of disappearing from view altogether. It is an admirable expression of a great deal of research. Its only limitation is that some of the writing included is uneven in terms of quality. This is not surprising given the aim to gather together as many voices as possible from the various regions. One hopes too that the Heinemann African Writers Series – ghettoised as it usually is by mainstream reviewing practice – will provide the anthology with an adequate home.

Nail it Clean

by Harry Clifton

JOHN FULLER

Stones and Fires

Chatto and Windus, £7.99,
ISBN 0 7011 6327 5

AS NADEZHDA MANDELSTAM tells us in her memoirs, her husband became depressed when stars started appearing in his poems. It was a sign that "the tailor's material was running out" and nothing was left of the original impulse now but cold abstraction. There are stars and star-gazing in John Fuller's poems, but they are some of the warmest, most human presences in a book where technique, like a spacecraft, is constantly negotiating the big, cold spaces left too open by abstraction and generalisation.

The most ambitious sequence in the book, a set of twenty-two sonnets called 'Europe', showcases both the virtues and the problems. The good, of course, is Fuller's willingness to step outside insular Englishness and Europeanise his concerns, in this case the first Balkan war of 1991. Less good is the excessive length with which he does so, a problem which recurs throughout the collection, as well as his tendency to adopt a kind of Audenesque voiceover, intoning human and political generalities over a crossfire of loss, atrocity and warfare in the foreground. Number eight, a potted history of Balkan origins, gets the mix of general and particular more or less right –

> The Turk at length withdrew like a tired lover
> And all Vienna breathed into a waltz,
> Informers blown to pieces with their cover
> And emperors forgiven with their faults,
> Religions left on rocks like prison islands
> And borders argued over like old toys,
> Resentments manoeuvring in utter silence
> And townships breaking up in dirt and noise.

– but too many others end up as slickly-versified common decency, playing off abstraction against abstraction –

> A resolution will not force compassion.
> Pain makes no contribution to ballistics.

> No interested government can fashion
> occasions of weeping out of cold statistics

– and so on. As a whole, 'Europe' hovers somewhere between Auden's 'Sonnets from China' and more recent anti-war poems by Harrison, Hulse and Shapcott. But it is stronger on ethics than poetic immediacy.

It seems no accident, however, that 'Europe', with its attempt at a larger engagement, is dated "Corsica, August 1992". For the South, the Mediterranean, seems to nudge Fuller out of the bloodlessness that dries up too many of these poems, turning them into exercises in style, with no pressure of feeling behind them, no real reason why they should have been written in the first place. The pseudo-meditative air of 'The Garden' is a case in point:

> If others care to overlook these long
> Endeavours, let them, for after all we are
> Contented merely with corroboration.
>
> The solemnest face caught staring in would be
> Your own. The reason that it never is
> Seems like the reason for almost everything.
>
> We are, possibly, posed this riddle early
> In life: which is the likeliest of mirrors,
> The face that reflects the world, or another face?

There is any amount of this psychic doodling, cloned out of Wallace Stevens in his weakest manner, but without his hypnotic enjambments that at least keep the mind shuttling back and forth on a musical loom, even when the sense is lost. A radical pruning of this stuff would have helped, and if, instead of playing the spinet in the parlour, Fuller twanged his Hank Williams guitar in the woodshed a bit more, a welcome note of profanity might have come through. For behind the Oxonian, there if a balladeer trying to get a look in, and when he does, things liven up. One of the best poems in the book is the short, raunchy 'Barbed Wire Blues' –

> how's that wild thing getting in?
> Keep him out with 4 Point 1 Between,
> Roll me 4 Point 1 Between, yes, and nail it clean,
> My baby has the tightest little snatch you ever seen.

– and when he takes his guitar south to the warm, fragrant Mediterranean it seems to free up his id a bit, with some entertainingly louche results as in 'Canicule', a poem about last year's heatwave as lived through on the shimmering Corsican littoral. For a moment MacNeice, in his gunslinging Streets-of-Laredo mode has elbowed aside Wallace Stevens at the bar.

But these are splashes of colour in a grey monotone. 'History' is the kind of poem one reads out of duty. So are 'Interrogations' and the slightly Hughesian black humoresque 'Logical Exercise' with its strings of generalisations. To paraphrase Percy Lubbock on bad fiction, the reader is always being *told* things he should feel or believe, rather than being *shown* anything. Fuller has an irritating habit of ascending too quickly out of the "I", the personal experience such as it is, into the didactic "we", and lecturing from on high on the great verities. This is from 'Looks':

What are we left to stare at but ourselves?
Absorbing absences with infinite mass,
Night with no stars that are not out of sight,

Areas of dangerous collapse where we
Are nothing again, as once upon a time
We were and some time yet again will be.

The pose of assumed wisdom is one he escapes from only rarely. Part of the problem is that the limited experiences on which the poems are based are reamed out excessively. When the padding is removed, as it is in short lyrics like 'No More', 'Two Galleries' and 'Shape', there is a true terseness.

There are books which ask to be read by the mind, as there are those best read by the heart, or even the body. This is one for the mind, and like many books filtered through intellect, it benefits from re-reading, from a kind of conscious application. No-one takes away more than two or three poems from most collections, and apart from the ballads, the one that stayed with me out of this one is its final meditation, 'Star-gazing'. Again, it is very long, but this time with a music, like Stevens' 'Man with the Blue Guitar' that draws the reader in rather than excluding him. And the most human sides of Fuller – Corsica, wine, the life of the body awake or in sleep, and memories of a dead father – combine to infiltrate the simple, though hypnotic metric with a lambency that is warm and personal at last:

Alpha Centauri in the night
Look down and tell me what to think.
Pour out unstinting, as I write,
Over my intermittent ink
Your steady undistracted light.

Here, the stars really *are* "the tailor's material". For once, perhaps, even Mandelstam may have got it wrong.

Dab Hand

by Ian McMillan

GLYN WRIGHT
Could Have Been Funny
Spike Books, £4.99,
ISBN 0 9518978 4 5

NOW THIS IS A GOOD THING: a genuine new voice from a genuinely new press, suddenly rushed to the front of the queue by the magical kiss of being a Poetry Book Society Choice. Nice precedent: let's build it into the PBS's constitution that at least one quarter's choice each year is given to a new writer from a new press, and then we won't slip back into the bad old days, when I first joined the PBS (in my school uniform) and it almost felt like everything that was any good was being published by Faber or Oxford. Not that they didn't publish new, good, work . . . Let's not get into that argument.

Glyn Wright is living evidence of the nurturing power of a strong local workshop and reading network; he's a major part of the hotbed of literary activities that flourish in Liverpool and this gives his work an unpatronising sense of audience, something that so many poets, digging away in their lonely allotments, never achieve.

The work is designed to be read aloud but has none of the perceived two-dimensionality that woolly thinkers often associate with perfomance poetry. Wright wants his work to have linguistic depth as well as oral felicity, and he's created a kind of plain language that sings. Here's his 'Bricklayer':

"This is just another wall. / His trowel dabs muck / over each brick end, hand slaps the brick in place, and ringing tool whips off / squashed muck, flicks it down / by his concreted boots". The language follows the movement of the craftsman, in the same way that a Matt Simpson poem might, and in 'Mrs. Mop' Wright celebrates, like Simpson does, the uncelebrated, as a wife waves her husband off to war: "When I heard of his posting I ran to the dock, / stood with young wives on the ferry's top deck / waving to one man lost in two thousand".

This isn't to suggest that Wright is a lost brother of Simpson's, swapped at birth, just that he's aware of antecedents. The Liverpool Poets are all here too, but Wright has processed them through his own mill and come up with something new and fresh. He isn't a wisecracker or Lee-Evans-on-the-page, but at the end of the book you come away with a smile on your face at the sheer humanity of the man, and how many poets can you say that about ?

It's fascinating that this humanity shines through even though some of the subjects of the poems are people you wouldn't want to meet on the street, like the satellite dish owner, parading his little bit of knowledge: "I bought the dish with my pay-off, got the biggest / the roof would hold. There's a lot of domes in Kabul / and different militias. And the tribesmen in New Guinea / wear penis sheaths and rub mud on their bodies . . ."

Wright has now got to work towards The Difficult Second Collection, the one that's tripped up a lot of poets in the past (it left me reeling, for one) but I've got faith in him, faith in his monologues, his images of work, his declarations of love. All together now: three cheers for the PBS! Hurrah! Caps in the air!

GLYN WRIGHT
TO THE WIND

Alleyways smell of piss and bones, of yesterday
and years ago. Pavements are covered in footprints
you can't see, where all the dead people walked.
But once I found a stone with silver speckles.

I've slept out on the wasty where blackbirds nest;
bowls of mud and soft dry grasses, four speckled eggs.
You get big winds down there, tasting of salt
and ice, but there's places you can crawl inside.

On walls you get hate in different colour paint.
Down alleys you get bickering and vendettas,
men picking bones over pitch and toss, lumpy
greenies where throaty ones have gobbed.
You get dog and bottlenecks and last week's news
and kick-the-can lads shooting up.

Silver is precious, can be stretched into thread,
and if it were a sound would be like a melody.

I make my lips round and do the blackbird tune
and dream of no more tit for tat, no more
gauntlet or racket, no more smack or crack;
never again the loggerheads or daggers drawn.

Don't Forget Your Ego

by Judith Palmer

Talking Verse: Interviews with Poets

eds. Robert Crawford, Henry Hart,
David Kinloch, Richard Price,
Verse, £10.00, School of English, The University,
St Andrews, Fife KY16 9AL
ISBN 1 872612 059

CHANNEL 4'S LATE NIGHT game show *Don't Forget Your Toothbrush* contained an unexpectedly riveting round, pitting a pop-star against his number one fan in a frantic race to discover who knew more about the star's life. Each week a succession of hapless celebrities stood trounced, unable to recall any of the critical facts of their own lives. Song titles, chart placings, band members, favourite ice-cream flavour . . . their fingers froze over their buzzers in dazed horror. Was this what their lives amounted to? The fans meanwhile romped on to certain victory, pouncing confidently on each piece of trivia: no, no, the years immersed in the minutiae of another's life had not been in vain.

And is a zealously-prepared *Verse* interviewer so very different?

"You've described Reznikoff as one of the few poets in whose work 'the imagist (of the moment of existence) and the narrative (of the timespan) co-exist'. How do you feel the two co-exist/have evolved in your own work, particularly the poem sequences?" asks Ken Cockburn of Tom Leonard. "I couldn't really answer that, at least I wouldn't want to", replies Leonard tersely. "It's up to the work to answer that, if it can. It's not up to me to start giving assessments".

In his introduction to *Talking Verse*, Robert Crawford writes of the magazine's aim to acquire interviews, "confident that these would be of both contemporary and, later, of considerable historical interest". For over a decade, *Verse* has indeed proved an invaluable resource, as the twenty-six contributions reprinted here testify. There's a Scottish emphasis, but the scope is wide-ranging, interviews with established poets such as Tony Harrison and Sharon Olds, sharing the pitch with start-of-their career conversations with younger writers like Glyn Maxwell and Kathleen Jamie.

The magazine's eye on posterity has, at times however, worked against itself. Line-by-line glosses of specific poems or interpretations of essays are doubtless of scholarly interest to devotees, but watching critics indulge in literary trainspotting makes a less-than-compelling spectator sport.

Give a poet a freer rein, however, and the result is far more interesting, as Frank Kuppner wryly acknowledges in his spoof self-interview. "I refuse to be sidetracked", insists the interviewer, doggedly pursuing his own line of enquiry. "Then you will never be a poet", his quarry replies. "In fact, that could almost be a definition of poetry. The ability to be sidetracked down many roads at once".

It is in the sidetracks, the byways and the muddy footpaths of *Talking Verse*, that the poets best reveal themselves. Ask Les Murray why he prefers the poetry of Garioch to MacDiarmid, and he'll explain via a scenic ramble comparing his cousin's funeral with poet Ken Slessor's: "He was not famous for anything much, old Hughie, except that he'd fallen off his horse once on an heirloom fiddle, and he used to take lots of live lizards to school in his pockets. That was all he was famous for, but he drew eight hundred, and the party lasted for two days after it, you know. That's how to do it".

The real pleasure of the volume is hearing each poet's distinctive voice emerge as they run with a subject close to their own hearts: Matthew Sweeney on food for example, Joseph Brodsky on the literary canon, Simon Armitage on lists, Dana Gioia on new formalism, or Liz Lochhead on the difference between writing for the page and performance. There's plenty of fascinating biographical detail and random facts, plus some excellent reflections on other poets, often jauntily expressed, as with Don Paterson on imitation "Muldoonery", poets "playing Cliff Richard to Muldoon's Elvis – they've perfected the hip-swivel and the curled lip, but somehow you just can't buy it".

With over twenty separate interviewers at work here, *Talking Verse* lacks the unifying authorial voice of, say, Clive Wilmer's *Poets Talking*, making it one to dip into rather than read through methodically. The book's layout, sadly, is puritanical to the point of sadism; with the closely-spaced type offset directly from the magazine, and varying somewhat, as *Verse's* style changed throughout the years. A little updating on the biographies and a word on the interviewers wouldn't have gone amiss.

Once braced to do battle with the print, however, readers will find *Talking Verse* a book of frequent pleasure and surprise illuminations, whether driven by a prurient thirst for personal detail, scholarly interest, or a love of language and the quirky aside. I suspect most of us side with Amy Clampitt, who admits, "Like most bookish people, I've been drawn to whatever I could learn of the lives of the writers whose works thrilled me".

Talking Verse features interviews with: Fleur Adcock, Simon Armitage, John Ash, Joseph Brodsky, John Burnside, Amy Clampitt, Mark Ford, Dana Gioia, Lavinia Greenlaw, Tony Harrison, W.N. Herbert, Kathleen Jamie, Frank Kuppner, Tom Leonard, Liz Lochhead, Angela McSeveney, Glyn Maxwell, Edwin Morgan, Les Murray, Sean O'Brien, Sharon Olds, Don Paterson, Robert Pinsky, Matthew Sweeney, John Tranter, Gerard Woodward.

Still Fishing

by Dennis O'Driscoll

W. S. GRAHAM

Selected Poems

Faber, £9.99,
ISBN 0 571 17659 3

WHEN W. S. GRAHAM died in 1986, his brief obituary in *The Times* appeared under a longer one for the founder of the Ross frozen foods empire. J. Carl Ross had owned a large trawler fleet and made a vast fortune from processing fish. W. S. Graham, whose best-known (though certainly not his best) poem is 'The Nightfishing', had lived frugally in a borrowed cottage in Cornwall. Processing fish into fish fingers is, needless to say, a more profitable enterprise than processing fish into poems; but the very process by which language communicates became a source of fascination and inspiration for W. S. Graham.

Some poets are lucky in their contemporaries; others are devoured by them. Graham, most unusually, could be said to have drifted from the second category into the first. To begin with, he was so besotted by the melodic tongue-twistings of Dylan Thomas (his elder by just four years) that he echoed his master's voice; yet, the very struggle to break free and "to speak what I think is / My home tongue" made him the highly original poet he became: one as conscious of the unstable nature of language as any deconstructionist.

Graham's apprentice poems, published in the early Forties, read as though they had been couched in a wartime code so impenetrable as to confound his allies no less than his enemies. Over the following decades, he abandoned the murky seawater of those poems, their lines collapsing like waves, for the kind of clearwater clarity found in 'Loch Thom':

I have come
Back to find Loch Thom maybe
In this light does not recognize me.
This is a lonely freshwater loch . . .

Despite his long years among the painters of the St. Ives school (his finest poems include elegies for Bryan Wynter, Roger Hilton and Peter Lanyon), Graham's work is much more aural than visual. The first word in the *Selected Poems*, "Listen", is an important injunction for Graham as he tunes the reader's ear to hear everything, even silence: "The ear says more / Than any tongue".

Graham's best work has a great density and rhythmic force, as if the flow of his language had been dammed for the purpose of generating the maximum power. A witty and playful poet, flitting nonchalantly between the abstract and the concrete, he is always aware of the artifice of art and the tenuousness of every utterance: "I am beginning to have nearly / A way of writing down what it is I think / You say".

Whatever doubts Graham may have harboured about the possibilities of communication, his later work consistently engages the reader at both the emotional and the intellectual level. This *Selected Poems* does far more justice to his inventive talent than the one which Graham himself (with too much wistful thinking about his early work) approved for publication by The Ecco Press in 1979. While the bulk of the contents is drawn from the *Collected Poems*, it also contains a few uncollected items (though not the small heartpiercing masterpieces of his last years: 'The Alligator Girls', 'The Fifth of May' and 'Alice Where Art Thou'). W. S. Graham's following, like Basil Bunting's, is remarkably diverse; admiration for his work links such different writers as Harold Pinter, Carol Ann Duffy and Michael Schmidt. Despite this, his readership is still inexplicably small and the fact that he is a poet of genius remains a better-kept secret than it ought to be.

Same Difference

by Deryn Rees-Jones

SHARON OLDS

The Wellspring

Cape, 1996, £7.00,
ISBN 0224 04351 X

IN *THE WELLSPRING*, Olds' fourth collection, we find her exploring by now familiar ground: yet this time around her own sexual experiences and childhood memories are more clearly juxtaposed with her experience as a mother watching her children's development from childhood through adolescence. Many of the poems read, not unexpectedly, as celebrations of heterosexuality – which is all well and good – except for the feeling that Olds seems surprisingly willing to surrender the difficulties of male / female relationships to a blanket philosophy of love. What exactly *are* the implications of the desire she expresses in 'Lifelong' to be

> . . . the only
> woman for a while, and love the entire
> human in the man?

Difficulties again in 'The Source' when Olds writes "I didn't know if it was a sickness or a gift. / To reach around both sides of a man" to

> . . . help guide the massed
> heavy nerve down my throat until it
> stoppers the hole behind the breastbone that is always
> hungry,
> then I feel complete.

If it takes a penis for a woman to feel complete then is Olds implicitly saying that without one women feel *incomplete*? This seems an old argument to dredge up, but surely what Olds needs to be saying is that it's an expression of sexuality that might make a woman feel "complete" (and even that seems a strange word to use), and that penetration, and the desire for penetration are, or may be, a very important part of that – but surely not all? And isn't the image of a sexually insatiable woman very different from an image of a woman who is powerful and happy in her expression of sexuality? In 'West', a poem which appears in the last of the book's four sections, Olds writes that she has "always wanted to cross over / into the other person, draw the / other person over into me",

> to meet men
> fully, as a woman twin, unborn,
> half-gelled, clasped, nothing
> between us
> but our bodies, naked and when
> those dissolve
> nothing between us

Is this a kind of Platonic rewrite or does it espouse a more radical politics of sexuality? Hard to tell, but in the same poem (which gives a peculiar slant on Plath's 'Lady Lazarus') Olds figures herself eating the ashes of her cremated father – an image she used to much more subtle effect in *The Father* (1993) – and seemingly enforces, rather than questions, a mystical relationship between men and women of power and forgiveness. Tricky ground, this, and to be fair to Olds, it is only because she *is* brave enough to explore the dangerous areas of gender, love and sexuality that these problems arise. Nevertheless, such a careless use of imagery is emblematic of the way Olds' work can stumble from a valid exploration of sexual politics into a dismaying conservatism.

In a recent *Verse* interview Olds has spoken of the personal being universal, but the trouble is that Olds is a "personal" poet (and, if I understand her correctly, Olds seems to make the distinction between that and any idea of confessionality) whose experience is very much situated in a white, North American experience of dentistry and junior proms. So while much of Olds' work will remain moving and important because of the way it transgresses taboos of experience and language, to pretend that it can transcend any notions of cultural, racial or historical difference seems, at best, naive. In 'Her First Week' there is an exquisite portrait of the first week of a child's life – "I looked at her and she swivelled her slate / eyes and looked at me. It was in / my care, the creature of her spine . . . / as if the history / of the vertebrate had been placed in my hands"; but it is those poems in *The Wellspring* that recount the dailyness – rather than the miracles – of middle-class life which work less than well,

lapsing even into the solipsistic and sentimental. This may seem harsh, but Olds' increasing dependence on the often astonishing clarity and power of her voice, without an equally intense use of figurative language, fails to allow us as readers to *re-experience* all that she appears to want us to: the grief, the loss, and perhaps, most importantly, the sense of surprise.

Deryn Rees-Jones' book of essays, *Consorting with Angels: modern women poets*, is published by Bloodaxe in Spring 1997.

Short Reviews

Louis MacNeice, *The Strings are False,*
Faber, £7.99,
ISBN 0 571 11832 1

The MacNeice boom goes on, with Faber reissuing Edna Longley's *Louis MacNeice: a Study* and the *The Strings are False* along with Jon Stallworthy's biography in paperback. *The Strings Are False* is one of the 20th century's best-kept secrets: a wonderfully nimble piece of prose and one of the best accounts of life in the 30s. Don't be put off by the subtitle, "an unfinished biography". It is a substantial book, covering the first 33 years of MacNeice's life, i.e. to the watershed of 1940 and his return to Britain after a stay in America. *[PF]*

Otto Orban, *The Blood of the Walsungs: Selected Poems,*
Bloodaxe/Corvina, £6.95,
ISBN 1 85224 203 5

Orban's prose poem 'Europe' begins "I have always backed off from the word", but in English translation at least the Hungarian Orban comes over as very European. 'The Apparition' invokes "the whole piss- and blood-smelling novel / which Central Europe works up". Born in 1936, Orban was indelibly marked by the war in which his Jewish father died in a camp. His poetry is savagely sardonic: 'The Ladies of Bygone Days' takes an unusually entropic view of former lovers: "they all live somewhere on the earth live well live poor no need to worry energy is conserved". The strongest poems are the unrhymed sonnets which cross Central Europe with Lowell and Berryman. *[PF]*

Arthur Rimbaud, *A Season in Hell & Other Poems,*
trs. Norman Cameron, Anvil, £8.95,
ISBN 0 85646 220 9

Like J. B. Leishman's translations of Rilke, Norman Cameron's Rimbaud versions have retained their appeal. The pungent, bitten-off quality of the originals is there: 'Your hates, your stubborn torpors, quick abandonments, / And the brutalities endured long since, you wreak / Them all on us, O night, yet with no ill intents, / Like an excess of blood discharged at each fourth week" ('Sister of Charity'). Cameron's translations were orignally published in two books, *Selected Verse Poems of Arthur Rimbaud* (1942) and *A Season in Hell* (1949). Also included here is a previously uncollected translation, 'The First Communion', which first appeared in *Poetry Review* in 1949. *[PF]*

John Hegley, *Love Cuts,*
Methuen, £8.00,
ISBN 0 413 69910 2

John Hegley's fifth collection gives us another view of his suburban world, populated by dogs, Dads and scouts and dominated by religion, short-sightedness and self-deprecatory childhood reminiscences. Hegley's poems, which he has described as "heavy light verse", don't work quite as well on the page, but only because his performances accentuate his eccentric wit. Hegley defies definition as *either* poet *or* comedian – his work entertains, and this book is no exception: the internal rhymes surprise and the final lines often act as punchlines: "I'm sore / I've got love no more / I'm sore / I'm a hinge with no door / and no screws". *[MD]*

National Poetry Competition 1995 prizewinners

THE JUDGES FOR THE 1995 COMPETITION WERE PAUL MULDOON – WHO IS THE POETRY SOCIETY'S NEW PRESIDENT – U. A. FANTHORPE AND ANDREW McALLISTER. THE PRIZEWINNERS ARE JAMES HARPUR FOR HIS EIGHT-SONNET SEQUENCE 'THE FRAME OF FURNACE LIGHT', SIMON RAE FOR 'THE TORTURER'S BREAKFAST' AND CHRISTOPHER NORTH FOR 'ROUGH PASSAGE'.

First Prize – £4,000

JAMES HARPUR
FROM: THE FRAME OF FURNACE LIGHT

Visiting

It could be the departure lounge at Athens:
Sound-proof glass, anxious Arabs, Greeks, swept marble.
Only the deep lifts hint at any menace.

Within the silent maze of corridors
My mind winds up as I close in on my goal
Dry-mouthed like Theseus sensing the Minotaur.

Room 303 – there he is! Half man, half bed,
Bellowing with laughter, his blubbery belly
Quivering above the sheets, his twitchy head

Ablaze with pre-op nerves and quickfire jokes,
A bull tycoon as helpless as a puppy
Eager for pats and reassuring strokes.

At length I leave. My unravelled mind is led
From trail to trail, but cannot keep the thread.

Second Prize – £1,000

SIMON RAE
THE TORTURER'S BREAKFAST

consists of freshly squeezed orange juice
thinly sliced ham
and some grated Parmesan cheese.

He is tired. His work is hard.
He has been at it all night
under the bare bulb
that hurts his eyes.

He's under-rated. No appreciation
of his subtlety, his intuitive sense
of when to ease off
and when to go on
through the screaming.

His marriage is on the rocks.
His hours are unsocial,
his love-making apologetic.

He suspects an irrational jealousy
of all the other flesh
that passes through his hands.

She says she can't talk to her friends.

Think of the pay, he urges.

The pay, she shouts back at him,
hardly covers the laundry.

Third Prize – £500

CHRISTOPHER NORTH
ROUGH PASSAGE

The captain on the bridge believes he is two
                                                people.
No he doesn't, he believes he's three people.
No he doesn't, he believes he's a seagull.
No, not a seagull, two dolphins;
no, three dolphins;
no, two dolphins and a porpoise
or is it two people and a porpoise?
Or three people?

Packing crates barge about the lower deck;
we do not like the growing list to starboard.
From the bridge comes a high peewit whistle,
then a thunderous foghorn
then the ship's bell giving three rings,
then two, then four. We can see no horizon.
We notice the creak of rope in the life-raft
                                                davits.
Seagulls careen across the grey sky
and two porpoise flop onto the aft deck.

Now there are three captains
who each believe that they are the only captain
but who secretly know that one of the other
                                                two
is a real captain but they don't know which
                                                one.
No, they know which one but won't say.
No, they know which one but don't like him.
No, they truly believe there are two captains.

Sorry, three captains.

The 1996 National Poetry Competition will be launched in May. The judges are Paul Durcan, Jo Shapcott and Paul Hyland.
For an entry form send a stamped addressed envelope to:
National Poetry Competition Organiser, The Poetry Society, 22 Betterton Street, London WC2H 9BU.

Tapping into Europe

by Michael Hulse

HARRY CLIFTON

Night Train through the Brenner

The Gallery Press, hbk £8.95, pbk £4.95
ISBN 1 85235 123 3 (hbk), 1 85235 122 5 (pbk)

HARRY CLIFTON COMMANDS my respect for several reasons. One has less to do with his poetry than with his presence: he is almost invisible. This is not a matter of hieratic aloofness. Clifton is a lover, not a despiser of people. But he sets no store by the gratifications of a circuit where poetry is equated with rock'n'roll. In him there is a temper similar to that of Horace in the sixth satire of the second book, where the poet is richly aware of the value of secluded quiet, and regrets the waste represented by city chit-chat, duties and bustle. This is my second reason for respecting him, and it is germane to his poetry: Harry Clifton has an unusually clear sense of the still centre of the turning world, that centre where those few things are that matter to him most. His centre, like Hemingway's Paris, may be a moveable feast – recent years have seen Clifton, a Dubliner, living in Italy, Germany and (currently) France, and many of the poems in this collection see him in transit – but wherever he goes a firm sense of self remains at the core, aware of exile (nowhere more sharply so than in Dublin) but above all celebrating the knowledge that home is where you choose that it shall be.

It might, for instance, turn out to be at an Italian standpipe:

There are taps that flow, all day and all night,
From the depths of Europe,
Inexhaustible, taken for granted,

Slaking our casual thirsts
At a railway station
Heading south, or here in the Abruzzo

Bursting cold from an iron standpipe
While our blind mouths
Suck at essentials, straight from the water table.

The thirst in Harry Clifton is a real and seemingly unquenchable one, for clarity, for purity, for access to the ancient source. It is only water that he drinks, of course. But no, it is not only water, it is history:

Where are they now, those ladies with the vapours
Sipping at glasses of hydrogen sulphide
Every morning, while the pumphouse piano played

And Russian radicals steamed and stewed
For hours in their sulphur tubs
Plugged in to the cathodes of Revolution?

Real cures, for imaginary ailments –
Diocletian's, or Vespasian's.
History passes, only the waters remain,

Bubbling up, through their carbon sheets,
To the other side of catastrophe
Where we drink, at a forgotten source,

Through the old crust of Europe
Centuries deep, restored by a local merchant
Of poultry and greens, inscribing his name in Latin.

The movement of Harry Clifton's mind, from standpipe to pumphouse to Diocletian and back, is characteristic: elsewhere he has Dante and electric trains in a single stanza. The history he wants is the history that will make sense of his own presence where he happens to be, and for the pertinacity of his quest for it I respect him too.

But I have been using a word that may seem cool, "respect". It is a word that seems only rarely to be used in poetry reviewing, as if there were no longer a ground on which minds could meet; but it is to precisely that meeting that Clifton's poems move. That movement is structured by a firm intellect, no doubt, but it has fire to it as well, so that we think of Derek Mahon's praise: "There must be three things in combination, I would suggest, before the poetry can happen: soul, song and formal necessity. Clifton has all three". It is in his poems of love (and his tussles with the philosophers – but those may be an acquired taste) that we see all three working in most cogent harmony. Plain Clifton is, but without that yobbery that often mars plainness; complex he is, but without the superiority that makes complexity ugly; and he inspires something that goes beyond respect:

I said to myself, even then –
Male wholeness, contemplate
The luck you have, with your casual pen,
The luck you may never have again,
Your work, which is also play,
Your house, for which you have not paid,
The new and sacramental light
You see your wife in, maidenly flesh
Accepting you, on the afternoon bed,
Desirable, affectionate,
In short, the miraculous heights
You have raised yourself to, of late –
I wrote it down, one day,
While the knowledge was still fresh.

It is revealing that in this last of the four stanzas of 'Abruzzo' there are so many words – "house", "miraculous" and "knowledge" in particular – that invite us to ponder implications, and it is important that those implications are matters not of accident but of substance. Harry Clifton plays only serious games with words. My guess is that he must draft poems many times indeed, since his work bears all the signs of fortunate discovery and meticulous craft; but in his discoveries there is nothing fortuitous, nothing that would lead away from a known understanding, just as in his craft there is nothing that does not contribute, cogently and often movingly.

Harry Clifton taught in West Africa and worked with refugees in Thailand before returning to what seems a very simple kind of life in Europe, dedicated to writing but not to the vanity encouraged by promoters. The tone that has resulted in his poetry is an extraordinary one. It possesses unusually combined qualities of modesty, firmness of mind, rhythmic integrity and sheer devotion (to his art, to his ideals of human conduct, and to the bride with whom he balances bottles of wine in the train). When, like Clifton in the last poem here, you're thinking what to take and what to leave behind, be sure to take this book.

HARRY CLIFTON
REDUCTIO

"I could spend the rest of my life simply drawing a table and two chairs".
– Alberto Giacometti

What is big? What is extended in space?
Not this studio, surely, not this glass
On a wooden table, or the apple
Trapped forever in the intersecting planes
Of redemptive vision. Certainly not this face –
But the rue d'Alesia, outside in the rain,
The millions of strange people
Whirled like atoms through the hub of Montparnasse

As night comes down, and the lit conceptual cages,
Dome, Select, Rotonde, the stamping-grounds
Of seeing and being seen, the gilt cafés
And mirrored brothels of the rue de l'Echaudée,
Where goddesses file naked on the stage,
Invite appraisal, and your mind's hot foundry
Casts them in bronze, remote as steles,
Cycladic or Sumerian, ancestral but still real.

What is big? What is extended in space?
Not the little tin soldiers, oh so small
In toyshop windows, though they say it all.
Not the yellow decals, not the pedestrian lights,
Stationary Man, or Walking Man, in the night's
Electric statuary. Not the living gaze
Forever fugitive, but only the skull;
The pleasure-seekers after hours, crashed out

On benches and late metros, heads agape
In a staring void. *"All the living are dead"*
It suddenly hits you. No, not Woman now, not Tree –
And where did it get you, that theft of bread
In childhood? Not Paris now, but infinities
Of disconnected people, faces, times,
Humanity dissolving into shapes
At the ends of avenues, at the ends of rhymes.

What is big, now? What is extended in space?
A single tungsten bulb, a Palace-at-Four,
Your lean-to shed. Inside it, memory swarms
With ancient heads, in the depths of revolving doors
Beheld, forgotten . . . From table to wooden chair
Saharas spread. A glass suspended in air –
You take a drink. To keep your fingers warm
You busy yourself, with the one loved face
Attempted endlessly, with the one loved form.

Wisdom Enough

by Susan Wicks

GERALD STERN
Odd Mercy
Norton, $18.95,
ISBN 0 393 03879 3

IN ALMOST EVERY sense, Gerald Stern's recent collection gives us two books in one. The grouped poems of the first section, itself already quite meaty and substantial enough to stand alone, are followed by 'Hot Dog', a single poem almost 50 pages long that tracks the ghost of Whitman out into the streets of present-day New York City. The collection as a whole looks backwards over a painful transition, and forwards to a problematic but not unhopeful future. Not for nothing does the poet take us on a pivotal train journey between two cities:

> The pain was leaving, I could feel
> it leave. That was yesterday, the end
> of January, 1991; today
> the sun is out.

Janus is one of the many human deities that, implicitly or explicitly, preside over this book.
Gerald Stern is not an easy poet, and, for some-

one unfamiliar with his work, *Odd Mercy* might not be the easiest place to begin. Any barriers there are, though, are not at the level of language, which is almost invariably simple. Nor are they, really, a product of the idiosyncratically comprehensive frame of reference which slips from Benjamin Franklin to Puccini to Nixon to Horace and back again without apparent strain. It is Stern's teasing, understated logic which forms the backbone of these poems and which makes them so tantalising:

> For all that grackles are despised
> I saw a baby grackle
> walking on the red leaves
> around my Honda.

For a moment we are almost in Lewis Carroll country, where birds and animals have a strange wisdom, where choice is a dangerous business – where the logic of syntax itself provides the only usable key. The door swings open on riches: a landscape of backyard birds and flowers gives on to the cultural life of cities, ordinary people, the disenfranchised. This is the complex, hard-earned vision of an older poet, accompanied by a good dose of self-irony:

> Still like a child, isn't it?
> Climbing up an iron staircase,
> arguing with some Igor
> over the broken lock
> . . .
> "Softened by time's consummate plash",
> isn't it?

Everywhere in these poems there is a powerful sub-text of bewilderment and loss, a winter of human relationships – and trust in an eventual emergence. There is humour too. If the poems often sing, they also do something much less harmonious, much more rueful and self-deflating. The poet is:

> a kind of
> cross between a toucan
> and a sparrow, doing his laments
> at the top of his voice, his false one
> to be sure, stabbing his wives
>
> one by one – a specialty –
> making his savage speeches,
> writing his bitter letters
> on his legal pads.

Yet the few poems about the death of the poet's mother are moving as only Stern's blend of simplicity and indirectness could be.

Stern's world itself is double. Everywhere there is a preoccupation with opposites – bluebirds streaked with red, the body of a cat dried to something resembling a leather football, the burning bush that cuts and burns its discoverer, the dead plucked cockerel in the "debonair", "nineteenth-century" armchair. But these are not abstractions. Just as the bluebirds, cardinals, grackles and doves that inhabit these pages are also real birds with bright eyes and feathers and heartbeats, so Stern's search for wholeness is at the same time individual, specifically Jewish and universally human: "I can trace / my eyelids back to central Asia". If we follow him, so, almost, can we.

The often surreal juxtapositions are, finally, liberating. And this is the special grace of Gerald Stern's poetry: "loose" and apparently informal as it is, it is nourishing as the best poetry can be. We are used to searching for the "poem to end all poems". And these are "poems to begin all poems". *An Odd Mercy* is shown us. It is January 2nd as I write this.

All Titles and Tenderness

by Matt Holland

TESS GALLAGHER

**My Black Horse:
New and Selected Poems**

Bloodaxe Books, £8.95,
ISBN 1 85224 306 6

Portable Kisses

Bloodaxe Books, £7.95,
ISBN 1 85224 365 1

WHERE EMILY DICKINSON was neat, numeric, but unseductive, Tess Gallagher is precise, poetic, and inviting: in titles. Reading down her six Contents pages is an unexpectedly moving and at times complete experience. Titles like hers are in danger of telling too much. Away you go, seduced by words, making pictures in your head, and being struck by "remembrances of your own highest thoughts" when titles like these leap off the page. 'Words Written Near A Candle', 'Love Poem to Be Read to an Illiterate Friend', 'The Same Kiss After Many Years', 'My Mother Remembers That She Was Beautiful', 'Some With Wings, Some With Manes', 'If Blood Were Not as Powerful as It Is', 'Their Heads Bent Towards Each Other Like Flowers', 'Now That I am Never Alone', 'We're All Pharaohs When We Die', 'To Whom Can I Open My Heart?' and 'Don't Wipe Your Madness Off Me'.

As you come to the last one, lean back to draw breath, or to ponder, you wonder if the poems will deliver what their titles promise. Gallagher has given herself a problem that Dickinson neatly avoided.

But first, before you can answer that question, by reading the poems drawn from five collections dating back to 1976, there are two cracking bits of prose to enjoy. The flyleaf quote from St Teresa tells us where the poet is coming from. "Words lead to deeds . . . They prepare the soul, make it ready, and move it to tenderness". And there's plenty of that in Gallagher's work, chiefly the tenderness of relationships. The next dozen pages, titled 'My Father's Love Letters', offer the kind of insights into the workings of the poet's mind that we rarely get in introductions to collections by British poets, if we are lucky enough to get an introduction at all. "I want to begin with rain . . . It is the climate of my psyche . . ." explains Gallagher. Of course, if you are a reader who is first detached and suspicious before being open and charitable, then this is no insight for you, and will amount to mere metaphor and psychobabble. But for those who like it, there's plenty more, about "the freedom of the spirit", words as "the tools of home-making" and poems as "acts of a prolonged beginning". There are echoes of Hughes and MacCaig in all this. Maybe something to do with life spent on the land, near earth and animals during formative years.

But when it comes to the poems, the feelings in the best of them are universal. As in the following, where title seamlessly runs into first line.

BEGINNING TO SAY NO

is not to offer so much as a fist, is
to walk away firmly, as though
you had settled something foolish,
is to wear a tarantula in your buttonhole
yet smile invitingly, unmindful
how your blood grows toward the irreversible
bite. No, I will not

go with you. No, that is not
all right.

Where at all possible, Gallagher likes to say things simply, often in single-syllable words. Peter and Jane at Primary School would have little trouble with any of the words in 'When You Speak to Me', and might even enjoy a chat about meaning in the first verse:

Take care when you speak to me.
I might listen, I might
draw near as the flame
breathing with the log, breathing
with the tree it has not
forgotten. I might
put my face
next to
your face

in your nameless trouble,
in your trouble
and name.

Trouble is not troublesome to Gallagher. Nor are words, which seem to work harder for her the shorter they are. Long titles, short words, good poems. Read them. Get tender.

Tender and enticing enough titles, but perhaps not quite the words promised to follow them, are found in Gallagher's next collection, *Portable Kisses*, which she says she wrote "as a fresh breath" when it was "time to get on with life" after the death of her husband Raymond Carver. "I wanted a book that could be read in the bath, a book perishable as certain kisses, which must be eagerly, even a little recklessly renewed". Which explanation alas is in danger of blowing away the magic of kisses in a way and for the same reasons that many of the poems do: it says too much, explains well but not too wisely, makes rational words direct instinctive actions. In recommending and articulating "reckless renewal" Gallagher has adopted the late-night sex counsellors' approach, one remedy for all and all for one remedy. There could now be a sudden rush of reckless kissing (carefully planned, of course) by readers of slim volumes. Ah, if only all things were as utterable in words as some people would have us believe! But then doves kiss brilliantly and coo about it too.

In further explaining her reasons for writing these poems, Gallagher says "I wanted a mixture of love poems and poems pointedly reserved for representing kisses". Well, on textual evidence she gets the latter but not much of the former. In fact, a novice or a veteran in matters of love could read this collection and wonder where love was, unless by love she means "the West's wide realm of general wit, tenderness and play between intimates . . . [with the kiss in all this] yearning for the full range of human foibles". Come to think of it, that could be one of love's many meanings.

Read a certain way, as celebration rather than explanation, the shorter they are the nearer these poems get to the love bit in kisses. 'Little Invitation in a Hushed Voice' has all the tenderness of a song of innocence, and experience.

Even birds help
each other. Come
close. Closer.
Help me
        kiss you.

But when they are long something goes wrong, kissobabble takes over, love of lips becomes love of logic, metaphors go mad, the notions and theories pile up. Take this, from 'Kiss Without a Body':

You think I don't know life
humbles us to its measure?
How the magnet of beauty
                        tears
at the skeleton, aging it
from the inside out?

or this:

The Kiss of the Voyeur
is made of lingering.
While the kisses of others
tear greedily the pages of the
                        face,
she uncloaks against time,
                        against breath,
against memory.

Gallagher is keener to explain the kiss than describe it and thus risks murdering to dissect. She seems a million miles from Neruda's *Veinte Poemas de Amor* and Lorca's *Romancero Gitano*, both of which collections of love poems she cites as inspirations. Maybe something to do with the northern hemisphere logician's longing for a bit of the loose-limbed language, of passion, that is a natural part of even everyday speech in more southern parts. We are as our land and our air is, said Gertrude Stein. And Wittgenstein: of which we cannot speak we should pass over in silence. Kissing?

Matt Holland is Director of the Swindon Festival of Literature.

Huddersfield on Sea

by James Keery

MILNER PLACE
In a Rare Time of Rain

Chatto & Windus, £6.99,
ISBN 0 7011 6251 1

HAVING DISPLACED LONDON as "the poetry capital of England", the Huddersfield Gang has made strategic advances on the metropolis itself, which, since the capture of Faber and Chatto by 'Lucky' Armitage, has been braced for the fall of *Poetry Review*. "Peter Forbes had better start looking for a nice pub to retire to", warns Poetry Business godfather, "Handsome" Sansom, while reviewers have received courtesy calls from Geoff "The Hat" Hattersley and Mac "The Knife" McMillan.

Fearless and incorruptible, I was going to praise this poet anyway, honestly. Milner Place is a native of North Yorkshire, and a *bona fide* Huddersfield resident. Hattersley's Wide Skirt Press published his first English pamphlet collection in 1989, when the poet was in his late fifties, with a collection in Spanish to his credit already (*En Busca de mi Alma,* 1977). *The Confusion of Anglers* actually sold out and was reprinted in a more stylish format the next year, followed by *Where Smoke Is* in 1990. *In a Rare Time of Rain* contains only four poems from those collections, excluding even 'Atlantis', in which the poet imagines the sunken city

> always two fathoms
> below the diver's
> aspiration
> always beyond
> the next field
> of kelp

Those lines still strike me as perfect, sustaining comparison in their quiet way with Constantine's astonishing rendering of the inundation in his classic of the same name. The pattern of indentations and wavering anapaests and dactyls enact the movement of seaweed in water, as the rhythm obliges the reader, like the diver, to draw breath after "aspiration". As well as the indrawing of breath, "aspiration" denotes both ascent and desire, mirrored in the descent and disappointment of the diver.

In a Rare Time of Rain consists of a number of undistinguished lyrics, interspersed with six longer poems: two seafaring narratives and two formally similar pairs. 'The Log of the Sloop Exceed' fails to live up to its title, but 'The Cruise of the Spy', a found poem based on the account of a South Shields slave-trader, effectively exploits the woodenness of its source – "Poor creatures! What distress they / showed! Some thought we lived upon the sea and they our fare" – and purveys some exotic commodities, such as the brandy that failed to tempt the African king "till / we stiffened it with cayenne peppers". Alas, it's holed below the waterline by piratical clichés, as when the Captain, "his knuckles white / on the handle of the cat", "curled up his lips, shot / / venom from his eyes" and "flogged / a female captive to the bone".

'Lum Street' and 'Costalago' are sequences of mocking mini-sagas set in the Pennines and the Americas respectively, indebted to *Under Milk Wood* for silly names such as Lucrece Hepmondwike and Cuthbert and Ariadne Weekes and addicted to titular double-takes ("SAM LOWE AND BILLY BRIGHT WERE DROWNED / / out by the Salvation Army Band"). Both have their moments, as in the portrait of Jeanie MacPherson the fishmonger: "Her legs, though much admired, seemed out / of place amidst a multitude of fins".

'Top Hold' and 'Charlie Ottoway' make use of the Align Centre command, like so:

> I sometimes think I shouldn't
> have left Concepcion Delgado for that sulky flamenco
> dancer.

The musings of a British salt, who can smell his long-lost dog when he comes in out of the rain, 'Charlie Ottoway,' would have been more moving if it weren't marred by cadences and cutenesses reminiscent of Muldoon, a contagion caught perhaps from Armitage. The most intriguing poem in the book is 'Top Hold', which takes an Audenesque overview of an imaginary civilisation in a protean but primarily South American environment, whose beauty and fragility are depicted with disquieting irony:

> though as far as vultures
> could make out there
> swam a sea of green, even

sloths were uneasy,
subject to fits
of animation. Turtles

and long-nosed dolphins
became disorientated . . .

In a Rare Time of Rain can ill afford the omission of 'Atlantis', but it's worth having if only for those animated sloths.

James Keery's first collection, *That Stranger, The Blues* , will be published by Carcanet in July.

MILNER PLACE
STRANGE FRUIT

Just now the music's
in the rain and in
the washing of the trees,
but when the light
fell on the roofs
and idle chimney-stacks,
it sounded like a band
of Irish pipes supported
by the wail of trains.

I would not wish to die
in such a breaking of a day,
on such a note,
but in the music of the rain,
now that's another thing,
with a score written
by those hands
that carved out flutes
and conjured fire. That
is the river that we run,
dance to be danced
deep in a forest
where the flowers thrust out
their genitals with greedy lips
and curl their phallic tongues,
or in the jig-sawn streets;
cadences of stone,
arias of roots
and steel.

Music's a fine way
of seeing things, just as
a trumpet sounds like brass,

and violins become the voices
of bent pines, and drums
are rumbling stomachs
of wild beasts, palpitations
of fear-stricken hooves,
blues are the harvest
of the cotton fields.

Strange fruit,
mood indigo,
rain-wash on leaves,
a dying day,
chorus
of equinoctial geese,
a full moon drifts
behind a hanging tree.

Half Cock

by Stephen Burt

ROBERT CRAWFORD

Masculinity

Jonathan Cape, £7.00,
ISBN 0 224 04371 4

ROBERT CRAWFORD'S PREVIOUS books, *A Scottish Assembly* and *Talkies,* sketched Scottish identity in a style derived equally from journalistic acts of noticing and post-Ashbery indirection. The best of *Masculinity* replicates that achievement; if this were a first book its Scottish-themed work ('Two-Line Poem', 'Incarnation', 'Recall') would be reason enough to announce a new talent. But most of the rest of these 54 short poems are ultra-clear testimonials to the author's unease about gender and his happiness with his wife and young child; almost every one of those poems is a let-down. The title lyric traces a boy's education (erotic and literary) through a charming grammar of fumbles:

That term I became her Latin lover,
My whole world zinging with testostericity,
All I touched shocked by another language –

Trees, ships, houses, horses, roads
Masculine or feminine, caressed
And confused, the way next term Greek

Gendered things just a little differently,
Maybe because it was older.

At once pathetic, serious and funny, this is the peak of Crawford's new style. More typical are the first lines in the book:

My best friend at school, then at university
Turned out to be gay

Which was fine, but left me somehow
Lonely. I knew I'd never

Be a ladies' man, or a man's man either.

Why re-read this, other than as prose autobiography? These lines seem sad, politically dodgy ("I'm not gay" is their first implication) and typical of Crawford's use of flatness and honesty as disarming effects – the same effects that sank John Berryman's *Love and Fame,* and which generate exactly the kind of thin, plot-driven work Crawford's older poetry surpassed.

A lot of these poems are maddening because parts are so unassumingly *good;* the same one that ends with the Pharisaic smugness of "Show me that scene in *Thunderball* / where James Bond changes a nappy" envisions a sperm as "a speargun-carrying, tadpole-flippered frogman / Whose visor fills up with tears". The fluent comic lists of 'Lochs' are worth £7 alone:

> Loch Transit gurgling through domestic pipes,
> Loch Radiator Coolant, Loch Tear, Loch Soup,
> And then the ones we mustn't talk about,
>
> The wee wee lochs in underwear, Loch Sweat
> Only dogs drank at, far
>
> Loch Alcoholism, sunny and serene,
> With just the possibility of rain.

"Wee wee?" – Crawford loves to pile up domestic artifacts – turnips, cardigans, kettles, sleeves. Sometimes these souvenirs celebrate the persistence of scrappy, hidden traditions, whether of childhood or of Cambuslang. But in the poems of marriage and fatherhood nothing in the lists seems endangered, or exciting; reeling off their names is ever *too* comfy. The bleakest of all lists is 'Next', instructions for a world in which all labour, even pregnancy, is alienated:

> Count the trees on Prince Edward Island;
> Set the economy to rights;

> Give birth; meet the new sales targets;
> Eat more fresh vegetables; work nights.

This – and other skewed, politicised catalogues, like 'The Numties' and 'Consumptive' – should stick in the memory in ways the confessional poems ("My psychiatrist was reassuringly normal") never will.

But these are experiments, departures. If parts of this book point back to *Talkies*, or forward to stranger lines, the parts that reflect the title point nowhere. It's not equality, or even sensitivity, if doing your half of the dishes is still something to write home about; self-congratulation for being so honest undermines the New Man poems even more than their flatness. An *ars poetica* to Crawford's father explains: "My job to know you there and know the knowledge / Doesn't interrupt me, nourishes what I do . . ." That's one, rather cozy, notion of how poets describe their world. In another, poets *are* interrupted, by knowledge that isn't guaranteed to assure us the ways we live are right or best. One hates to seem ungrateful for displays of tender happiness, but it might be better for Crawford's poems if whatever they take on next agitates him more.

Stephen Burt writes for the *TLS* and *Thumbscrew*.

DON PATERSON

IMPERIAL

> *Is it normal to get this wet? Baby, I'm frightened* –
> I covered her mouth with my own;
> she lay in my arms till the storm-window brightened
> and stood at our heads like a stone
>
> After months of jaw jaw, determined that neither
> win ground, or be handed the edge,
> we gave ourselves up, one to the other
> like prisoners over a bridge
>
> and no trade was ever so fair or so tender;
> so where was the flaw in the plan,
> the night we lay down on the flag of surrender
> and woke on the flag of Japan.

NEWS/COMMENT

CAFE ONLINE

Throughout the winter building work has been going on to transform the basement, ground floor and first floor of 22 Betterton Street into the Poetry Place, with an Internet suite, cafe, and seminar room, thanks to £99,000 worth of Lottery money and additional funding. The cafe opens on 8 May.

It joins a great tradition of literary cafes and cafe-bookstores such as the Globe and Beefstew in Prague, Cafe Centrale in Vienna, and the philo-cafes in France. Restaurateur Mark Mitchinson, formerly of Mars in Covent Garden, aims to create just such a continental cafe atmosphere with a Polish vodka freezer and newspapers as well as literary magazines available for browsing. A key feature of the Poetry Place will be the basement reading room with Internet stations and materials for writing. The Place will be a feature of the updated Poetry Map at http://www.bbcnc.org.uk/online/poetry, so you can visit us by computer wherever you are.

The Poetry Place is open to all Members and Friends of the Poetry Society, who can sign in up to three guests each. The basement and upstairs room can be hired for launches and events. Booking is advisable for meals at the Poetry Cafe (Tel. 0171 240 5081). *Speechless at the Poetry Cafe*, a monthly open reading session, starts on Tuesday 21 May at 7.30 pm. No advance booking. Readers should arrive at 7 pm and sign up on the door. £3 or £2 concessions.

With the rich heritage of the Poetry Society in mind, cafe diners might like to chomp through 90 years of poetic history. Here are a few suggested tasters:

Waste Land Waffles (1909-1948) – no, not the perfect accompaniment to a cup of Prufrock's coffee, this rather amorphous dish celebrates a long period in which nothing very much happened at all.

Stopes's Jelly (c.1949) – rumoured to have contraceptive properties. Marie Stopes was a Council Member of the Society when Muriel Spark was Editor of *PR*. The two had ding-dong battles.

The Old Bob Cob (c.1975) – sour dough baps filled with macrobiotic alfalfa emit the cry 'Bunting' when bitten. Thrill to the flavour of a colourful era when the permanent avant-garde, poets like Eric Mottram and Bob Cobbing, led the traditionalists a merry dance.

Motion's Marmalade (1982-3) – a delicately Oxonian conserve. A brief fashionable interlude marked by a delicate, elusive flavour.

Brownjohn's Butty (c.1985-89) – a homely, austerity style Hovis sandwich with a hint of Romanian spices. It was Alan Brownjohn's vision of sandwiches in the bar that led directly to today's Poetry Cafe.

Barker's Bun (1989-93) – strictly for bunfights. The Society was at this time famously fissiparous.

NET VERSE

Each quarter Peter Howard conducts a brief surf of poetry on the World Wide Web, dropping in on some of the coolest hot-spots.

Time was, you'd load a Web page and be sure there'd be a soft grey background, readable black text, and links to other sites in nice bright blue. But no self-respecting site would be seen dead in grey this season. Strong primary backgrounds are in vogue with those pages that haven't turned black in protest at the US Communications Decency Act. The Poetry Society's page **http://www. bbcnc. org.uk/online/poetry** (which has reasons of its own to be concerned about what can and cannot be safely published in cyberspace) is out on the catwalk with the best of them. Some useful info here and a nice poem from Fleur Adcock, though it's a pity the links page is in eyestrain red.

Kicking the trend is the Bristol Poetry Page **http://www.ssynth.co.uk/~rday/poet** which uses all the resources that modern technology offers to produce a virtual exercise book. Lots of good info, though, particularly if you live around, er, Bristol.

Those in the Smoke may prefer the *Poetry London Newsletter* page **http://metro.turnpike. net/P/poetry/index.html** which maintains details of poetry venues and events.

Also slickly constructed is LIVING POETS **http:// dougal.derby.ac.uk/lpoets/** one of the best e-zines I've spotted, with some good, ecstatic stuff by Philip Wells.

If you're not satisfied with just one e-zine, try John Labovitz's list **http://www.meer.net~johnl/ e-zine-list/index.html** which contains hundreds, on all sorts of subjects. It's recently gained a subject index, which makes it a lot easier to find things than trying to guess from the titles what they're about.

A page that isn't on a lot of links, but ought to be, is the Shakespeare archive **http://the-tech.mit.edu/**

Shakespeare/works.html Not only does this contain the Works, but it also has a search engine that finds every occurrence of a word or phrase you enter, and can bring up the plays and/or poems it occurs in. Serious scholars and those just wanting to look up their favourite quotations will find it invaluable.

E-mail me with your favourite (or unfavourite) sites via peter@hphoward.demon.co.uk or look up my own page **http://ourworld.compuserve.com/homepages/Peter_Howard/** which has links to all the sites mentioned, and more.

MOVING ON

Alert readers of the prelims of the *Review* will have realised that over the last 5 years the magazine changed from one man band to team effort. The last 4 issues have been produced by a troika of the Editor, Martin Drewe and Rachel Bourke. Rachel is now moving on to be an Account Manager at Pell & Bales. Rachel was the first person at the Poetry Society in the last ten years (other than the Editor) to take seriously the job of selling the magazine and its advertising space. In one year she doubled the advertising income, and membership income, which is the bedrock support for the Society and *Review* alike, increased dramatically. She will be a very hard act to follow.

COMPETITION

The last competition series ran out of steam in Autumn '94, but enough readers missed it to ensure its reinstatement in our new regime. For Jessie Smith the comps were "delightfully quirky" and "I'd go so far as to rate the experience a mental orgasm". This makes setting the comps even more onerous than before – how can we let her down? – but we'll do our best. We aim to print at least three prize winners and each will receive up to three prime books of the quarter.

NO 1: ADVICE TO POETS

In his review of John Fuller on page 73 Harry Clifton suggests that it would be beneficial for Fuller's verse if "instead of playing his spinet in the parlour, [he] twanged his Hank Williams guitar in the woodshed a bit more". This is really useful practical criticism, unlike gawping praise or "this is crap" dismissal, it suggests a practical way forward in an admirably pithy manner. Similar terse, metaphoric and witty advice required for any poet who takes your fancy. Deadline June 15.

LETTERS

HARTLEY WILLIAMS'S DOTY
Dear Peter,

I don't know if it is worse to accuse a critic of being intentionally or unintentionally imperceptive, but John Hartley Williams' review of Mark Doty's *My Alexandria* (Vol 85 No 4) is either one or the other. I can't believe he used that oldest of reviewers' tricks, slating the writer for not achieving what he never intended to – see his complaint that a certain poem fails "to capture the essence of jellyfish". If the aim of this poem were to capture the essence of jellyfish, do you not think it might be called 'Jellyfish', rather than 'Difference'? Doty was trying to capture the essence, not of jellyfish but of imagery, a subject on which your man has some truly odd ideas.

Whenever he sees one of Doty's rich, allusive images, he wants to pin it down like a butterfly on a card, or reduce it to a mathematical formula – how, exactly, does x resemble y? But it doesn't always work as mechanically and simplistically as that. I recall, years ago, reading a line and a half of MacNeice to a rather dull group: "The bubbles in the football pools/ Went flat". . . . They pondered, and objected: "There aren't any bubbles in football pools". I took a deep breath and, I hope patiently, tried to explain that images don't just represent objects or ideas; quite often they also try to condense and telescope them, thus saying by means of allusion in a few words what would take a paragraph of prose. Bubbles occur in water; also in champagne which is used to celebrate good fortune; football pools give people the chance of making a fortune, but when the numbers don't come up, the hopes "go flat" like champagne bubbles . . . God, it's like trying to explain a joke, and has the same effect on the magic.

I felt I was back there when I read Williams' comment on the image at the end of 'No': "I think the children smell unopened, like unlit candles". How, asks your man, do unlit candles smell unopened? Well, let's see if we can't reduce this one to prose . . . First, Doty is clearly an expert gardener. This is relevant in several poems, and is incidentally the answer to another of Williams' tetchy queries, about a poem packed with detailed and exact references to plants: "why *Siberian* iris?" Because, pal, he *knows* one iris from another, and the distinction matters to him. Going back to 'No': young children's skin does, often, have a faint, fresh, characteristic scent, which might reasonably be likened to that of flowers in bud – i.e. unopened. But "unopened" also carries echoes of frequent partner-words, here unspoken – unopened letter, unopened present, unopened door. All potential, all unexplored.

And the candles? Well, the book is called *My Alexandria*, and despite what Williams says, Cavafy's sensual, elegiac presence is all over it. There's an overt pastiche, 'Days of 1981', direct quotes, and more subtle hints. Surely in such a book, "candles" has to recall one particular thing, the early poem which earned Cavafy his nickname "poet of the candles". Where he sees the years of his life as a row of candles, those behind him extinguished and smoking, those ahead still lit and glowing. "Unlit", to me, both echoes and subverts this image, by pointing out that even the lit candles – the future years – are, by definition, already burning away. The children are so young still, so all potential, that their future is still unkindled, hasn't begun to die.

If we must be mechanistic, it's a fact that unlit candles, especially scented ones, smell subtly different from the same candles lit, and again it's a distinction that might register with the sensitive nose of a gardener. But it's the wrong way to look at it anyhow. To return to MacNeice, you might as well ask how exactly musical notes can vanish like little fishes with a wink of tails. A mind like MacNeice's or Rilke's or Doty's makes more imaginative leaps than that.

We're all entitled to an opinion, and I normally wouldn't bother to argue, because usually it doesn't much matter whether people read a particular collection or not. But this one's different. When I first read *My Alexandria* I was feeling brassed-off with poetry, at least modern British poetry. I hadn't, for ages, read a collection that moved me, or that I couldn't easily have done without. Worse, the most admired and hyped collections were just the ones I disliked most, finding them smart-alecky and empty at the heart. Reading Doty, I made a perfect pest of myself, shouting "Class!" at intervals, quoting aloud, and, now and then, having to put it down because my hand was shaking. He was as much of an intellectual challenge as any fashionable clever young Brit, but he also challenged the emotions, which none of them will do for fear of looking naff. If some of them

hide much longer behind a screen of cool, "ludic" irony, they will vanish altogether up their own joky linguistic surface. They're fine at what they do; they make you think, but how often do they make you cry, the way Chaucer can, or Rilke, or Sorley MacLean – or Doty? I want poetry to do both, and I think it would be a damn shame if anyone missed out on this book because of your reviewer's myopia. Don't listen to him, folks; go out and spend seven quid. It's worth it.
Regards,
SHEENAGH PUGH
Cardiff

THE WINSLOW GIRL

Dear Poetry Review,

Bill Turner's review (Vol 85 No 3) of *Harvest*, Pat Winslow's collection of sonnets, displays an unbelievable arrogance. Many contemporary poets no longer feel bound to use the strict Petrarchan or Elizabethan forms. Some poets even mix elements of them together! Some even prefer to employ assonance or near rhyme because they enjoy the effect, not because they think all true rhymes "must be contrived". It's all a matter of taste, Mr Turner. It has nothing to do with "grunge technique".

I wonder how he would have reviewed the following:

Wordsworth's 'From the Italian of Michaelangelo'

pace/unbetrayed/grace/made
plea/thee
paid
imparts/hearts
dies hour/
power/flower/
paradise

(Whoops, haphazard rhyming pattern and a near rhyme)

Shakespeare's 'XXV'

stars/boast/bars/most
spread/eye/buried/die
fight/foil'd/quite/toil'd
belov'd/removed

(Whoops, two near rhymes and an unstressed rhyming with a stressed)

Marilyn Hacker's 'II'

cure/say/today/car
bed/before/cure/dead
speed/door/stay
did/four/away

(Whoops, more near rhymes)

Gillian Clarke's 'Marged'

bed/space/died/penniless
afternoons/glass/stars/tunes
car/cow/sycamore/too
garden/women

(Whoops, whoops, whoops)

Incidentally, I think poetry's pretty empty when read that way. Which only goes to show how important content is. Did Pat Winslow use the right words in the best possible order to get her content across? Buy the book and find out. I thought it was marvellous.
Yours faithfully,
LOUISE COODHAM
West Chiltington,
West Sussex

FOR A' THAT
Dear Peter,

A Quiz for you and your readers:
1) Which poet year by year effortlessly tops the lists of his nation's favourites?
2) Which poet is enthusiastically quoted by everybody, from the child in school to the old man in the pub?
3) Which poet is equally famous for his songs, one of which is on the lips of people well beyond the boundaries of his native land?
4) Which poet has had such an impact on his country's culture that his memory is enshrined in an annual social celebration?
5) The bicentenary of which poet's death was commemorated in January, but did not merit a single line in that quarter's issue of *PR* (vol 85 No 4)?
The answer to all the above questions is: ROBERT BURNS.
Yours sincerely,
JOHN KILLICK
Hebden Bridge,
West Yorkshire

A NOBLE COOLIE'S PRAISE
Dear Editor,

I was much encouraged to read Gwyneth Lewis's article on the art of translation(Vol 85 No 4). The technical, anecdotal and sociolinguistic points made cannot be faulted. I just found it a trifle ironic that such a marvellous essay had to travel from Wales to England via New York. One passage is especially memorable for a translator like myself: "I'm one of those who believes that not only is translation possible, it's an essential element in every nation's culture . . ."

I subscribe. The only problem is whether literary England is indeed open to outside influences. I am one of those pedants who immediately correct Dutch people when they call Great Britain "Engeland" which is habitual usage, but here I do mean England, even perhaps, Little England. Until recently, many English literary magazines tended to regard translation as something almost infradig unless it was done from Classical languages, where the authors are safely dead and there is plenty of leeway for "interpretation" (i.e. inaccurate translation, or Zukofskyian nuttiness). The tastes of the magic circle of monolingual editors have rarely been called into question. Let's face it, very few English editors (or other Brits. for that matter) can actually read anything in anyone else's language, 'O' level French proving to be a woefully inadequate tool to discover the delights of the literatures of others.

I fear that your mag, while not one of the worst by any stretch of the imagination, is not entirely innocent of the practice of keeping continentals at bay. Looking back over the list of back-numbers, I do see the heartening inclusion of such significant names as Czeslaw Milosz, Ovid, Joseph Brodsky, Irina Ratushinskaya, Ewa Lipska, Anna Akhmatova to mention just a few of the Europeans, let alone those from other cultures. However, poets from smaller languages are not so well represented; as regards Europe, only Romania appears to have been singled out for special treatment. Though rival Hungary has now been made visible thanks to George Szirtes with his Prizewinning Zsuzsa Rakovszky renderings.

What I should like to see in *PR* is a regular feature covering less well-known languages, not least in Europe. Theme issues are all very well, but tend to be like the Tom Lehrer song about National Brotherhood Week: if you "do" Europe, or the Caribbean, in one issue, you can afford to keep quiet about them for the next couple of years. The Netherlands and Flanders both Speak Dutch and though there are 20 million speakers of this language, living in countries whose coasts face Britain, I do not detect even one Dutch-sounding name among the eye-catchers mentioned among the back numbers. Also Scandinavian Poetry (c. 25 million speakers, including Finland) seems thin on the ground.

While I fully understand that the principal aim of *PR* is to present English language poetry to speakers of that same language, I cannot quite grasp why British and American literary magazines in general seem to publish a much smaller proportion of translations than say, the equivalent magazines from the rest of Europe, Western and Eastern. Since English is the world language, there is hardly any risk of what is inaccurately termed Anglo-Saxon culture being swamped, overwhelmed, or in any way threatened by the sensibilities of foreigners. The Achilles heel of British monolingualism is, luckily, the Celtic presence which prevents even the English from ever totally forgetting that most of the rest of the world speaks something other than English at home, whatever language they may use when presenting papers at international conferences.

It is also nice that the KGB is allowed to present its views on poetry, but again I feel it is the umpteenth time that Russians have described the horrors of the gulag mentality. Perhaps it is time for some of the other nations of the former Soviet Union and other Communist bloc countries to get a word in about how their poetry was stifled by Stalinism but tolerated later on. What about a "Letter from Estonia?" Jamie McKendrick, in his European Prize adjudication, is one of the few to acknowledge that even the Finns and the Portuguese have poetry (not just "primitive songs" as his fellow-judge would have it) and both gents mention Stanislaw Baranczak's renderings of Jan Kochanowski's elegies for his dead daughter. But who in the English-speaking world has ever heard of the brilliant neologistic genius of 20th century Polish poetry, Boleslaw Lesmian and his wistfully comic poem on the same theme? Kochanowski is an admirable start, but I would hope that the English one day discover the great wealth of Lesmian, Staff, Iwaszkiewicz, Norwid, Mickiewicz, Slowacki, Tuwim, just to name a few at random off the top of my head.

Yours faithfully,

ERIC DICKENS

Blaricum, The Netherlands

(*PR* Vol 85 No 2 had Dutch poetry on pp35–37 and a Letter from Estonia on p60 – Ed.)

SOME CONTRIBUTORS

Moniza Alvi's second collection is forthcoming from Oxford Poets.

Peter Armstrong's first collection, *Risings*, was published by Enitharmon in 1988.

Connie Bensley's latest collection, *Choosing to be a Swan* (Bloodaxe, 1995) was reviewed by Helen Dunmore in Vol 85 No 3.

Sujata Bhatt's latest collection, *The Stinking Rose* (Carcanet) was shortlisted for last year's Forward Prize.

Kate Clanchy's first collection, *Slattern*, was published by Chatto in January.

David Constantine's latest collection, *Caspar Hauser* (Bloodaxe, 1995), was reviewed by Michael Hulse in Vol 85 No 1.

Elaine Feinstein's *Selected Poems* (Carcanet, 1995) were reviewed by Judith Kazantzis in Vol 84 No 3.

David Gascoyne's *Selected Poems* (Enitharmon, 1995) were reviewed by Kevan Johnson in Vol 85 No 2.

Anthony Hecht's *On the Laws of the Poetic Art* was published by Princeton University Press in 1995.

Michael Hulse is currently completing a new book of poems, *Home*.

Gwyneth Lewis's *Parables and Faxes* (Bloodaxe) was shortlisted for the Forward Prize.

Edna Longley's *The Living Stream: literature and revisionism in Ireland* was published by Bloodaxe in 1994.

Gerald Mangan's *Waiting for the Storm* was published by Bloodaxe in 1990.

Roger McGough's latest collection is *Defying Gravity* (Penguin).

Jamie McKendrick's latest collection is *The Kiosk on the Brink* (Oxford Poets, 1993).

Kathy Miles's first collection, *The Rocking Stone*, was published by Seren in 1988.

Susheila Nasta is Editor of *Wasafiri*.

Cees Nooteboom is a Dutch writer well known for his fiction, which has been widely translated into English.

Judith Palmer is publicist for the South Bank Centre Literature Department and a Literature Officer at the Arts Council.

Don Paterson's second collection is forthcoming from Faber.

Neil Powell's biography of Roy Fuller was published by Carcanet last year.

Ruth Sharman has published in *London Magazine*, the *Sunday Times* and won 2nd prize in the 1989 Arvon Poetry Competition.

Jana Stroblova was born in 1936 in Prague. She published four collections before 1968 and was then unable to publish for ten years.

George Szirtes's *Selected Poems* are forthcoming from Oxford Poets.

Susan Wicks's latest book is *Driving my Father* (Faber, 1995).

Erratum

David Hartnett's byline in the last issue was incorrect: his *last* book was *Dark Ages* (Secker, 1992); his forthcoming book from Cape is still untitled.

Acknowledgement

John Whitworth's poem 'The Wild Good-Lookers' first appeared (*sans* illustrations) in *The Spectator*.